family field guide

— S E R I E S —

VOLUME THREE

Rocky Mountain Birds

written by
Garrick Pfaffmann

illustrated by
Hilary Forsyth

BearBop Press LLC

BASALT COLORADO USA

© 2008 all rights reserved
printed in China

Delta County Libraries

PO BOX 858
Delta, CO 81416
www.deltalibraries.org

family field guide
— SERIES —

field notes

field notes

ISBN-13: 9781882426287

Published by:

BearBop Press, LLC
www.bearboppress.com

Illustrated by:

Hilary Forsyth

Designed by:

words pictures colours graphic design

Distributed by:

WHO Press
www.whopress.com

Library of Congress Control Number: 2007943598

Acknowledgements

Thanks to the many people who graciously lent their time and expertise to help shape this book. Special thanks to John, Lindsay and Mason for their patience and to Jonathan Lowsky for his ornithology expertise. Thanks also to Judi Forsyth, Anne Siewert, Kelly Alford and Warren Ohlrich for their editing, designing and publishing expertise, respectively. It is a blessing to be surrounded by such talented people.

Author's Dedication

To people who look at birds
with fascination towards adaptation,
reverence for God's wonderful imagination,
and daily recognition of song, color, flight and survival.

Illustrator's Dedication

For all who delight
in watching the flight
of colors so bright
under the light of the sun.

Introduction

WHY BIRDS?

Without a doubt, birds are the most commonly observed wild animals in everyday life. Bird sightings are so common, in fact, that most go unnoticed. Because of their constant presence in our daily lives, birds provide a wonderful introduction to the study of animal behavior and their roles in local ecosystems. Mammal enthusiasts and wildflower lovers might drive to distant tracts of open space to see four-legged and flowering natives, but bird lovers need only peek out their window or tilt their heads skyward to satisfy their wildlife craving. This book is intended to add greater understanding of these everyday sightings.

GETTING STARTED

Watching birds at a backyard feeder or at active nests in the neighborhood is a great way to introduce an interest in birds. Remember, though, the beauty of birds is often small and subtle and acquiring an interest can take time. Not every bird watching experience is as captivating as staring eye-to-eye with a Great-horned Owl or watching a Bald Eagle pick a fish out of a slow moving river, so take time to enjoy and understand the bird encounters that happen right in the backyard.

MENTOR

Bird watching is a favorite past time for many people. Finding a knowledgeable person who can tell the stories of birds can help create an appreciation of their varied behaviors. Local nature centers and Audubon Societies often lead programs and events that can answer questions and tell the stories of local bird communities. Finding a knowledgeable mentor who can deepen the appreciation of our feathered friends is a key to continuing a fledgling interest in birds.

IDENTIFICATION WOES

Even after a decade of enjoying birds, I still struggle to identify most "little brown jobbers." Many small brown birds look identical and are nearly impossible to identify in the field. Don't let the difficult task of identifying these species get in the way of developing an interest in bird watching. Even small brown birds are fun to watch when they are feeding or building a nest, so don't get frustrated when you can't attach a name to the bird you are enjoying.

family field guide

How To Use This Book

Thirty-seven of the most commonly observed and easy-to-identify birds have been selected as an introduction to bird life in the Rocky Mountains. These common bird species represent a broad enough diversity of behaviors and characteristics to gain an understanding of bird life in this region.

BOOK NAVIGATION

While most scientific guides arrange the birds according to bird families, we have elected to list them alphabetically because it allows easier navigation for beginners. Users who know the birds' names and appearances can use the table of contents to navigate through the book. Users who can identify birds by appearance only can use the pictures on pages 10-11 to navigate through the book. Words written in *italics* are defined in the glossary on pages 94-95.

EASY IDENTIFICATION

The symbols, photographs and illustrations work together to teach bird identification skills. As described in the Bird Watching Tips on page 9, three keys to bird identification are recognizing a bird's size, habitat and outstanding features. The size symbol allows quick size comparisons, the habitat symbol and descriptions (in the appendix) relate species with site locations and the photographs and illustrations show outstanding features. A complete list of bird pictures is located on pages 10-11 for users who can identify bird features, but do not know the names.

BIRD BEHAVIORS

The symbols and text work together to describe bird behaviors. Symbols and a Habitat Chart on the left side of each page can be used to quickly understand each bird's nesting, migration and feeding behaviors. Other unique behaviors are described in the text or in captions below each photograph.

BIRD FAMILIES

The Classification Chart is included on the left side of each page for several reasons. First, it is fun to compare similar behaviors and features of related birds. Second, it is amazing to note the dramatic differences between relatives. Finally, most field guides arrange the birds according to families, so knowing the bird families and relatives allows easy navigation through other, more technical field guides.

Contents

family field guide

Bird Watching Tips

Watching birds can be as convenient as staring out the window at a bird feeder or as wild as track-ing bird calls in a remote wilderness. Use the tips below to improve the chances of seeing as much activity as possible and identifying what you see.

EARLY MORNING Songbirds are most active and most vocal one hour before the sun rises and in the next few hours before temperatures get too hot. Males of many species identify their territories each morning by singing to possible mates and to call off competing birds. Once daytime tempera-tures get warm, many birds feed quietly and are more difficult to locate.

SPRING AND EARLY SUMMER The full range of migratory birds arrives in the Rocky Mountain region by mid-May. They are at their most vocal and colorful during the spring and early-summer mating season when males are attracting their mates, defending their territories and while nest building is at its peak.

STAY A WHILE For the best results with any type of nature observation, it is important to find a comfortable spot and to sit or stand still for several minutes. After a person enters an area, birds and other animals go into hiding and become quiet. After a few minutes of quiet, however, the birds continue their natural activity and are easier to observe.

ECOSYSTEMS Each ecosystem provides unique habitat features for different bird species. To see a variety of species, visit a variety of different ecosystems. Birds often prefer to roost on the edge of two ecosystems where they can take advantage of a variety of habitat features.

IDENTIFICATION TIPS Because birds don't sit still like flowers and aren't as large as most mam-mals, bird identification can be difficult. Within a quick glance, successful bird watchers must notice the bird's size, unique features and its location.

SIZE The first key to identification is noticing the bird's size. Is it the height of a baseball, pencil, football or traffic cone? Use the symbols on each bird page to compare.

UNIQUE FEATURES Most birds in this book have colorful feathers somewhere on their body. No-tice any flashes of color and where they are located so that you can look at pictures later to positively identify the species.

LOCATION When observing a bird, take notice of where the bird is located. Birds tend to live in specific ecosystems depending on the season. Look at the life zone (elevation) symbols on each bird page, then look in the back of the book for more details to discover if the bird is likely to be found in the ecosystem where the sighting occurred.

family field guide

Quick Identification

Bald Eagle p.16

Cedar Waxwing p.18

Chickadee (Mountain) p. 20

Chickadee (Black-capped) p. 20

Clark's Nutcracker p.22

Coot p. 24

Dipper p. 26

Flicker (Northern) p. 28

Golden Eagle p. 30

Goose (Canada) p. 32

Gray Jay p. 34

Great Blue Heron p. 36

Grouse (Blue) p. 38

Hummingbird (Broad-tailed) p. 40

Kingfisher p. 42

Magpie p. 44

Mallard p. 46

Meadowlark (Western) p. 48

family field guide

Mountain Bluebird p.50

Nuthatch (White-breasted) p. 52

Osprey p. 54

Great-horned Owl p. 56

Ptarmigan p. 58

Common Raven p. 60

Red-tailed Hawk p. 62

Red-winged Blackbird p. 64

Robin p. 66

Sapsucker (Red-naped) p. 68

Steller's Jay p. 70

Cliff Swallow p. 72

Barn Swallow p. 72

Tree Swallow p. 72

Turkey p. 74

Vulture (Turkey) p. 76

Woodpecker (Hairy) p. 78

Woodpecker (Downy) p. 78

family field guide

Symbols

Look at the symbols on each bird page, then read the explanations below to understand their meanings.

WHERE Describes the life zones and elevations where the bird may live.

LOWLAND SHRUB AND FOREST LIFE ZONE (p. 86)

The Lowland Shrub and Forest life zone is located between 6,000 and 8,000 feet above sea level or up to 9,000 feet on sunny, south-facing slopes.

MONTANE LIFE ZONE (p. 88)

This life zone occurs from 8,000-10,000 feet above sea level and includes aspen groves, pine forests, douglas fir forests, wet and dry meadows and more.

SUBALPINE LIFE ZONE (p. 90)

The Subalpine life zone occurs from 10,000 feet above sea level to treeline. It includes engelmann spruce and subalpine fir forests, open meadows and more.

ALPINE LIFE ZONE (p. 91)

The Alpine life zone occurs only above treeline and includes wet and dry meadows, talus slopes and boggy willow beds.

RIPARIAN ECOSYSTEM (p. 92)

The bird nests in riparian ecosystems within the noted life zone. Riparian ecosystems occur on the land next to creeks, lakes, rivers and in wetlands.

SIZE Describes the bird's size. Knowing the size allows easier identification.

BASEBALL
The bird's height ranges from 3-6 inches tall.

PENCIL
The bird's height ranges from 6-12 inches tall.

FOOTBALL
The bird's height ranges from 1-2 feet tall.

TRAFFIC CONE
The bird's height ranges from 2-5 feet tall.

MIGRATION Describes the migration from summer breeding range to winter range.

NO MIGRATION
The bird does not migrate out of the mountains; it may migrate in elevation to find open water or less snow, but remains in the mountains through winter.

REGIONAL
The bird leaves the mountains to other parts of Colorado or neighboring states.

NEO-TROPICAL
The bird flies to southern states, Mexico, Central or South America.

FOOD Describes the bird's diet. The chart on the left of each page tells more details.

HERBIVORE
The bird eats only plants; nectar, seeds, leaves, buds or other plant parts.

CARNIVORE
The bird eats only meat; small animals, baby birds, eggs or dead animals (*carrion*).

OMNIVORE
The bird eats both plants and meat.

INSECTIVORE
The bird eats spiders, insect eggs, larvae and adults in flight, on the ground, on plants or underwater.

NEST Describes the bird's nest. The chart on the left of each page tells more details.

CUP-SHAPED NEST
The bird builds a cup-shaped nest with grasses, sticks, mud or other materials in trees or on cliff ledges.

CAVITY NEST
The bird uses a hole dug into a tree trunk or cliff wall; may dig its own hole or use an old one that has been abandoned.

GROUND NEST
The bird builds a nest on the ground, usually hidden among grasses, shrubs or fallen trees.

Common Bird Features

Most birds, except the Emu, Ostrich, Cassawary, Kiwi and Penguin, are designed for flight. Birds have feathers, hollow bones, toothless beaks and lay eggs to create lightweight bodies that are able to fly.

HOLLOW BONES

The heaviest part of most living bodies is the skeleton. Birds, however, have hollow bones which keep their bodies light so they can fly. Feathers are also a lightweight material, but the total weight of a bird's feathers is often more than its entire skeleton.

FEATHERS

Mammals have hair, reptiles have scales and *all* birds have feathers. Long, stiff tail and wing feathers are designed to move against the wind allowing birds to fly. *Down feathers* grow near the skin and provide warmth. *Contour feathers* cover the body providing warmth and protection from water and weather. Some contour feathers are brightly colored to attract mates, while others are camouflaged for safety.

EGGS

All birds lay eggs. Eggs allow new birds to grow within a safe, warm shell while the mother remains light enough to fly. As with mammals, the growing *fetus* inside the egg needs to be kept warm while it is growing, so a parent must sit on the egg 24 hours each day to keep it a constant, warm temperature.

NESTS

Most birds build nests to protect their eggs. Nests provide a soft place where eggs will not break, warmth to keep the babies growing and safety from predators. After the eggs hatch and the babies *fledge* (fly), most nests are abandoned unless they are used to lay a second or third set of eggs.

family field guide

Unique Bird Features

While all birds lay eggs, have feathers and hollow bones, each bird has unique features that have adapted to fit their feeding, flying and nesting lifestyle. Observing these unique characteristics leads to better understanding of a bird's behaviors.

BEAKS

The size and shape of birds' beaks are designed for individual lifestyles. Raptors have sharp, hooked beaks for tearing meat. Swallows have short, wide beaks for catching insects in mid-flight. Herons have long pointed beaks for grabbing fish from shallow water. Ducks have long, rounded beaks that reach to the bottom of shallow lakes. Every type of beak is designed for each bird's feeding method.

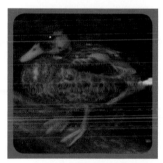

FEET

Birds' feet are designed for specific behaviors. Ducks have short, webbed feet for swimming. Herons have long, skinny legs for wading in shallow water. Cedar Waxwings have strong feet that allow them to reach for berries. Kingfisher feet are weak because they only perch on straight branches. Woodpeckers can swivel their toes to allow better climbing. For every different lifestyle, there are as many different feet.

WINGS

Wings come in different shapes and sizes to match each bird's flying needs. Hummingbirds have wings which flap in a figure-8 pattern allowing them to hover near flowers. Soaring hawks and eagles have flat, broad wings allowing them to soar on warm rising air. Swallow wings are V-shaped allowing them to turn quickly in mid-flight. Careful observation of wing design provides clues into a bird's behavior.

MIGRATION

In general, birds migrate to seasonal food supplies. Some birds migrate thousands of miles between their winter range and their summer breeding sites while others have a year-round food supply in their breeding habitat and do not migrate at all.

family field guide

Bald Eagle

PLACE	PLACE	SIZE

FOOD	NEST

MIGRATION	MIGRATION

National Park Service

CLASSIFICATION

SCIENTIFIC NAME
Haliaeetus leucocephalus

BIRD FAMILY
Eagle and Hawk family

ROCKY MOUNTAIN RELATIVES
Golden Eagle, Northern Goshawk, Red-tailed, Cooper's, Swainson's and Sharp-shinned Hawks and more

HABITAT

NEST
Built of sticks in sturdy trees; lined with mosses, grasses and their own feathers for softness and warmth.

FOOD
Mostly fish, but also ducks, coots, muskrats, turtles, rabbits, snakes and *carrion*.

MIGRATION
Short migrations to open water.

NATIONAL SYMBOL In 1789, the same year that George Washington became president, the Bald Eagle was elected our nation's official symbol. This designation did not come easily. Politicians debated for six years about which animal best represented our country's character. The majority of the Congress elected the Bald Eagle because it symbolizes strength, courage, freedom and immortality.

RIPARIAN HUNTER Bald Eagles depend on rivers, lakes and oceans for food. They soar high above the water or perch on tree branches watching for fish below. They can see shallow-swimming fish from hundreds of feet above the water. Once they locate their prey, they tuck their wings and dive at speeds up to 120 miles per hour (nearly twice the highway speed limit near most cities). As they approach the water, they spread their wings, drop their legs and dip their feet several inches below the water surface, trapping the fish in their talons. Bald Eagles are able to carry fish up to four pounds (equal to 16 Quarter Pounders) back to their perch where they eat. They may also steal fish from Osprey and they eat Prairie Dogs in winter.

BALD "Piebald" is an old word that refers to white patches of hair, skin or feathers. The Bald Eagle received a shortened version of the word which refers to the white feathers on its head.

family field guide

SUCCESSFUL RECOVERY

In the early 1900s, Bald Eagles were commonly shot. A law passed in 1940 outlawed Bald Eagle hunting, but their population continued to decline into the 1960's. Farmers were spraying a chemical called DDT on their fields which washed into streams, lakes and rivers. *Aquatic* insects absorbed the poison, then fish ate the insects and Bald Eagles ate the poisonous fish. As a result, Bald Eagles' eggs grew soft and few babies hatched. In 1967, The Bald Eagle was listed as an endangered species which forced the protection of the birds and their habitat. In 1972, DDT was banned in the United States and the Bald Eagle population has since improved. The Bald Eagle was removed from the endangered species list in 2007.

LONG-LIVED

If food is plentiful, Bald Eagles can live up to 40 years. Eagles which migrate long distances and work harder to catch food may live only 20 years.

NEST

Bald Eagles build huge nests in strong trees near water. Bald Eagle pairs mate for life and return to use the same nest each breeding season. Some nests are used by the same pair for over 30 years. Each year the pair adds more sticks to the nest which can grow to be 10 feet across (larger than a queen-size bed) and can weigh up to 4,000 pounds (heavier than a small car).

Nest If their nesting site is not disturbed, Bald Eagles return to the same nest each year.

Young Birds Bald Eagles don't grow white head feathers until they are four years old.

Cedar Waxwing

PLACE	PLACE	SIZE

NEST	FOOD	SPRING

MIGRATION	MIGRATION

CLASSIFICATION

SCIENTIFIC NAME
Bombycilla cedrorum

BIRD FAMILY
Waxwing family

ROCKY MOUNTAIN RELATIVES
None

HABITAT

NEST
Cup-shaped nests made of grasses, mosses and small twigs are usually placed in evergreen trees near berry-producing plants.

FOOD
Berries and fruits most of the year; insects in spring and early summer.

MIGRATION
Migrations range from the middle United States down through Central America.

FRUIT EATER The Cedar Waxwing is the most specialized fruit-eating bird in North America. *Frugivores* (fruit eaters) are rare this far north of the equator; most occur in the tropics where fruits grow year-round. In spring and summer, before berries are produced, Waxwings eat flying insects and small insects off of leaves, but in late summer, fall and winter they eat berries.

BERRY-BASED LIFE Waxwings' dependence on fruit affects several aspects of their lifestyle. While babies of most bird species hatch in spring or early summer, Waxwing babies hatch in mid to late summer, nearer to the berry producing season. While many species follow annual migration patterns, Waxwings fly to wherever they can find fruit in winter. Some birds return to the same place each season, but many flocks find different winter grounds each year.

WAXY WINGS The name Waxwing refers to small "droplets" of red which grow at the tips of the flight feathers. These red droplets have a waxy texture and are produced by the colorful cells (*pigments*) in their fruit-based diet. The bright yellow tips of the tail feathers are also affected by the pigments in their diet. A honeysuckle plant was introduced in the eastern United States in the 1960s which produces orange berries; Waxwings which eat these fruits while their feathers are *molting* have orange tail feathers rather than yellow.

EASY IDENITIFICATION

During migrations and in winter, Waxwings fly in mixed flocks with other birds. From a distance, Waxwings look like other hard-to-identify little brown birds. Their yellow tail feathers, however, stand out from other birds in the mixed flock. Once identified, their beautiful mask, wing and tail colors can be appreciated with binoculars.

AGING

Scientists can estimate the age of Cedar Waxwings by the size of the red, waxy "droplets" on their wings (above). Young birds have very small droplets while older birds have larger droplets.

CITY LIVING

Cedar Waxwings are common in urban areas where people are likely to plant crabapple trees and other berry producing plants.

CEDAR EATER

Juniper trees are a member of the Cedar family. They produce cones which are commonly called Juniper berries. These cones or "berries" are covered with a blue fruit and are a main source of food for Waxwings in winter when other berries are in short supply.

Face Mask Cedar Waxwings have a black mask across their eyes.

Tail Even two-week old babies have obvious yellow tail feathers.

Chickadee
(Black-capped and Mountain)

PLACE	PLACE	PLACE

SIZE	WINTER	SUMMER

NEST	MIGRATION

National Park Service

CLASSIFICATION

SCIENTIFIC NAME
Poecile atricapillus (Black-capped)
Poecile gambeli (Mountain)

BIRD FAMILY
Chickadee and Titmouse family

ROCKY MOUNTAIN RELATIVES
Tufted Titmouse

HABITAT

NEST
Mostly use abandoned woodpecker holes; may dig own holes in dead or soft trees.

FOOD
Insects in summer; seeds, fruits and fat from dead animals in winter.

MIGRATION
None; some move to lower elevations with less snow.

COMMON SIGHTINGS Chickadees are only the size of a third grader's closed fist, but they are easy to identify and are commonly seen. Their white breast and contrasting black head feathers are unique and obvious. They are commonly observed because they eat seeds from bird feeders and because they continue to perch on leafless branches in winter.

WINTER SURVIVAL While most songbirds migrate in winter, Chickadees remain in the mountains. To survive the cold temperatures, they fluff up their feathers trapping air close to their bodies. The trapped air becomes warmer than the outside air, which then warms their bodies. Chickadees also huddle close together under the protection of thick evergreen branches where they share body heat to maintain warmth.

TEMPERATURE CONTROL Food is difficult to find in winter. As a result, many animals find ways to use less energy during these cold months. Chickadees are able to drop their body temperature by nearly 20 degrees so that their bodies do not work so hard to maintain warmth. At this lower temperature Chickadees remain inactive, but are still able to fly if necessary.

NESTING Black-capped Chickadees may dig their own nesting holes in dried and rotten tree trunks, while Mountain Chickadees usually nest in abandoned woodpecker holes.

family field guide

BIRD FEEDERS

Chickadees are common visitors to winter bird feeders. If a feeder is used during these cold months, it is important to continue supplying food throughout the season as many birds become dependent on the household food supply.

COMMUNICATION

Chickadees are very "talkative" songbirds. They are known to make up to 15 different songs and calls which they use to communicate with other birds in their flock. Their call, *chick-a-dee-dee-dee*, is commonly heard by people because it is used to challenge intruders.

FOOD STORAGE

Chickadees eat constantly from dawn to dusk. Even when they are not hungry, they collect food and store it in cracked tree bark or beneath lumpy *lichens*. They may return to the storage sites later in the day or up to a month later. In winter, when food is less abundant, they depend on this "food memory" for survival.

PEST CONTROL

During spring and summer, a Chickadee's diet consists almost entirely of insects, caterpillars and spiders. Chickadees are considered one of the most important birds in controlling insect populations in evergreen forests and fruit orchards. In fall and winter, Chickadees eat seeds, dried berries and fat from *carrion*.

Donna Dewhurst   US Fish and Wildlife Service

Black-capped The Black-capped Chickadee has a solid black cap on its crown.

Mountain The Mountain Chickadee has a white stripe above its eye.

family field guide

Clark's Nutcracker

CLASSIFICATION

SCIENTIFIC NAME
Nucifraga columbiana

BIRD FAMILY
Raven, Magpie and Jay family

ROCKY MOUNTAIN RELATIVES
Gray Jay, Scrub Jay, Pinyon Jay, Magpie, Raven, Crow, Steller's Jay

HABITAT

NEST
Cup-shaped nest of twigs and bark is lined with grass and pine needles; built in evergreen trees.

FOOD
Mostly pine seeds, but also other seeds, nuts, berries, insects, *carrion*, eggs and baby birds.

MIGRATION
None; some migrate to lower elevation pine forests to gather and store seeds for winter.

MEMORY Clark's Nutcrackers survive winter by eating seeds which they have stored in the fall. Their beaks are specifically shaped to pull seeds out of pine cones. They have a special pouch behind their tongue, near their throat, which allows them to carry up to 100 pine nuts at a time to their winter storage sites. They store the seeds in thousands of different locations and are known to use rocks, trees and other landmarks to identify these storage sites up to nine months after they have stored them. Imagine hiding 1,000 Easter eggs on a hillside and remembering each location at the beginning of the next school year!

MUTUALISM The word *mutualism* describes a relationship between two species that help each other to survive, and in which neither species could survive for very long without the other. Clark's Nutcracker and pine trees have a *mutualistic* relationship; the trees feed the birds and the birds plant their seeds. Clark's Nutcracker is the most specialized pine seed eater of all North American animals. This is important because pine seeds are heavy and cannot move far from the parent tree on their own. A Nutcracker hides thousands of pine seeds each year, many of which are never recovered. While the Nutcrackers collect an entire winter's food supply from the pines, they plant many thousands of seeds in return.

family field guide

NON-MIGRATORY BIRD

Nutcrackers hide out beneath the protection of evergreen trees throughout winter storms. During this season when snow covers most food supplies, they eat the seeds that were collected in the fall. Because they have food, shelter and water, they do not need to endure a long and often dangerous migration.

EARLY BIRDS

Clark's Nutcrackers are actively breeding before migratory songbirds arrive in spring. They lay their eggs in early spring before the snow has melted from their surroundings. Once the snow melts and the babies have hatched, Nutcrackers begin eating insects and the eggs of late arriving migrants.

WILLIAM CLARK

Clark's Nutcracker and the Cutthroat Trout (*Oncorhynchus clarki*) are two discoveries made by the Lewis and Clark expedition that are named after William Clark. Most of their discoveries, including Lewis's Woodpecker and Blue Flax (*Linum lewisii*), are named after Meriwether Lewis, the scientific recorder of the expedition.

INCUBATION

Clark's Nutcracker is the only bird in the Jay family in which the male bird sits on the eggs until they hatch.

Beak The long, pointed beak is designed especially to pry seeds out of pine cones.

Differences Clark's Nutcracker (right) has a longer beak than the Gray Jay (left) and is much larger.

Coot
(American Coot)

FOOD   NEST

MIGRATION

CLASSIFICATION

SCIENTIFIC NAME
Fulica americana

BIRD FAMILY
Rail, Coot, Crake and Gallinule family

ROCKY MOUNTAIN RELATIVES
Sora, Virginia Rail

HABITAT

NEST
A platform of dried leaves floats on the water or at the edge of wetlands.

FOOD
Mostly plants; also insects, small fish and other small aquatic animals.

MIGRATION
Migrate to large, open-water lakes with shrubby protected shores.

OLD COOT Among duck hunters, the Coot is considered a pest and a distraction. It is inedible to most people, so to call someone an "old coot" is to label them an unattractive pest. Also, Coots make quite a commotion in their attempt to get airborne, running across the water and flapping their wings frantically. "Old coot" may suggest an old man who is slow to rise and reluctant to move.

FLOATING NESTS Coots live in marshy wetlands and along the edges of lakes where water is shallow and cattails grow tall. Cattails provide hiding places and nest building materials for Coots. Their nests are woven from dried cattail leaves and other marsh plants which float atop the water. In some cases, Coots build their nests on land immediately next to the water so they can quickly escape from land predators.

FLOCKING PROTECTION Osprey and Bald Eagles commonly prey on Coots in open water. When a flock of Coots identifies a predator, they huddle together in a tight formation in the middle of the lake. If the predator dives towards the flock, they flap their wings against the water creating a mad, splashing confusion that distracts the predator from focusing on any single bird. If the predator approaches a Coot, it dives several feet below the surface to escape the approaching talons.

family field guide

AGGRESSIVE EATER

Coots are omnivores, but they mostly eat water plants below the surface and in wetlands. They can dive 3-6 feet below water to eat plants in shallow lakes. If ducks are feeding nearby, Coots aggressively steal their food in an effort to maintain the best feeding places. They may even approach campers picnicking near the edge of wetlands and lakes in hopes of receiving a handout. Their aggressive, noisy nature, and even a knack for fighting with each other over food, may be the origin for the saying, "crazy as a coot."

FUNNY FEET

Coots look like ducks and they swim most of the day with ducks, but they belong to a family of birds that is built both to swim in open water and to walk through tall wetland plants. The main difference between ducks and coots is their feet. Coot feet are not webbed like those of ducks. Instead, they have four separated toes which allow them to walk quietly through tall marsh plants. Each toe has a loose flap of skin so their feet are partially webbed for faster swimming in open water.

RED EYES

While these birds appear to be entirely black and white, they have bright red eyes and a red spot at the top of their beak. These red markings are attractive, but are difficult to see as they blend in with the dark feathers.

MUD HENS

Coots bob their heads back and forth like chickens when they walk. Because they walk in muddy wetlands, they are sometimes called "mud hens."

Nest Coots use dried leaves and grasses to build floating nests in wetlands.

Mud Hens Coots swim and walk in shallow water and through thick, grassy wetlands.

family field guide

Dipper
(American Dipper, Water Ouzel)

CLASSIFICATION

SCIENTIFIC NAME
Cinclus mexicanus

BIRD FAMILY
Dipper family

ROCKY MOUNTAIN RELATIVES
None

HABITAT

NEST
Cup-shaped nest made mostly of moss; placed on ledges above the stream bank safe from floods and predators.

FOOD
Aquatic insects, small fish and fish eggs.

MIGRATION
None; some migrate to open water at lower elevations.

AQUATIC SONGBIRD American Dippers only live in and near fast-moving water. They are the only *aquatic* songbird in North America, rarely moving more than 10 yards from streams or rivers. Their nests are located on cliff ledges and under bridges near streams, rivers and creeks. They eat insects which hide beneath rocks in the water.

ADAPTATIONS While most water birds choose to survive in slow moving water, Dippers prefer to dive beneath fast-moving water. They use their wings like flippers, helping them to swim beneath the water's surface, then cling to rocks with their claws while digging for insects. They can only stay below water up to 15 seconds before coming back to the surface. Dippers have a thick layer of down feathers, a unique feature among songbirds, which provides warmth against the cold mountain water.

INDICATOR SPECIES A healthy Dipper population indicates a healthy river system. Dippers depend on aquatic insects which hide beneath rocks. They cannot survive in polluted rivers where insect populations are unhealthy or in areas where soil erosion is consistent enough to cover insects. For this reason, scientists observe Dipper populations as an indicator of water quality.

family field guide

QUIET SONGBIRD

Dippers use songs and calls to attract mates and to establish territories in spring, but they rarely rely on their song as much as other songbirds because of the noisy river environment. Their call is most often heard in mid-flight when they fly up or down the riverbed.

DIPPING

While standing on rocks in the middle of fast-flowing rivers, Dippers commonly bend their knees over and over again in a "dipping" motion. *Sibley's Guide to Bird Life and Behavior* suggests several theories to explain this behavior. First, dipping may be a way for the small songbird to show its strength and *dominance* to intruders. Second, dipping allows the birds to more accurately locate insects below the water. Other birds, including owls, often swivel their head up and down and side to side while focusing on prey.

OXYGEN

Animals need oxygen to survive. All animals inhale oxygen which flows to the heart and into the blood. The blood carries oxygen throughout the body allowing each muscle and organ to function. Dippers have cells in their blood that carry more oxygen than most land animals, allowing them to stay under water for up to 15 seconds without damaging their brains or other body parts.

Nest Dipper nests are made from moss and are placed above the flood line of rivers and creeks .

Food Dippers eat insects which hide beneath rocks in fast moving water.

Flicker

(Northern Flicker)

PLACE

PLACE

PLACE

SIZE

SUMMER

WINTER

NEST

MIGRATION

CLASSIFICATION

SCIENTIFIC NAME
Colaptes auratus

BIRD FAMILY
Woodpecker family

ROCKY MOUNTAIN RELATIVES
Lewis's, Downy and Hairy Woodpeckers, Red-naped Sapsucker

HABITAT

NEST
Make own holes in soft or diseased wood; line cavities with wood chips.

FOOD
Mostly ants and flying insects in summer; dried berries and seeds in winter.

MIGRATION
None; some migrate to lower elevations.

ANT EATER Flickers belong to the Woodpecker family, so they are built to climb up vertical tree trunks and to drill nesting *cavities* into them. It is unusual, then, that over half of their summer diet consists of ants, which live on the ground. Flickers have long sticky tongues like other woodpeckers, but instead of feeding on insects beneath tree bark, they dip their long tongues inside ant holes and pull out their food.

SUBURBAN NOISE Unlike songbirds, which use their voices to establish territory and to attract mates in spring, Flickers pound their long beaks on hollow logs, solid telephone poles or aluminum siding of houses. They choose whichever material creates the loudest *drumming* noise. The *drumming* behavior is often considered a nuisance in urban areas because the mating "call" occurs at sunrise, several hours before most people choose to wake up on their own.

WOODPECKER HOLES Flickers use their strong beaks to peck wood and to create a *cavity* nest in trees. Flickers are the largest woodpecker in the Rocky Mountains and their cavities are the size of a baseball. Other woodpeckers create golfball-sized holes. Each cavity is used for only one year, and a new hole is created each year. According to Janis Huggins in her book *Wild At Heart*, 40% of Colorado's birds use woodpecker holes for nesting, but only 8% of these cavity nesting birds are woodpeckers!

family field guide

HYBRIDS

Early scientists identified two different species of Flickers in the United States: the Yellow-shafted Flicker lived in the eastern states and the Red-shafted Flicker lived in the western states. In the mid-1900s, Flickers in the middle part of the country were observed with orange-shafted feathers. The Yellow and Red-shafted Flickers were mating and the offspring created a "new" species. Because the two orginal species mate so commonly, all Flickers are now classified as one species: the Northern Flicker.

NAME

The Latin name *auratus* means "golden" and refers to Flickers' bright underwing feathers. Northern Flicker flight feathers in the Rocky Mountains, however, are orange, not gold. Males flash their bright feathers in spring to attract females.

EGG LAYING

According to *Sibley's Guide to Bird Life and Behavior*, a researcher removed eggs from a Flicker nest each day, always leaving two eggs in the nest. The female continued to lay eggs each day to ensure that she had 5-8 eggs to hatch. By the end of the experiment, the female had laid more than 70 eggs in the season. Besides chickens, few birds are able to lay so many eggs in a single season.

Dave Menke   US Fish and Wildlife Service

Donna Dewhurst   US Fish and Wildlife Service

Markings The markings on the face, breast and back are unique from other woodpeckers.

Colors Yellow-shafted feathers occur in eastern states. Flickers in the west have orange shafts.

Golden Eagle

PLACE **PLACE** **PLACE** **PLACE**

SIZE **FOOD**

NEST **MIGRATION**

CLASSIFICATION

SCIENTIFIC NAME
Aquila chrysaetos

BIRD FAMILY
Eagle and Hawk family

ROCKY MOUNTAIN RELATIVES
Bald Eagle, Northern Goshawk, Red-tailed, Cooper's, Swainson's and Sharp-shinned Hawks and more

HABITAT

NEST
Very large cup-shaped nest built of sticks; placed in treetops or on cliff ledges.

FOOD
Small rodents, snakes, birds, rabbits, hares and dead animals (*carrion*).

MIGRATION
Short migration to lower elevations within neighboring states.

PROTECTED Ranchers in the early 1900s commonly killed predators which threatened chickens, ducks, sheep and cattle. Most carnivores including coyotes, wolves, bears and Golden Eagles, were considered pests by many people. Golden Eagles were placed under protection of the Bald Eagle Protection Act of 1940 because they look like young Bald Eagles. Today it is still illegal to kill Golden Eagles or to possess their feathers, nests and eggs.

VISION If the world's eight tallest buildings were stacked one on top of the other, and an eagle was standing at the top, it could look down to the ground two miles below and watch a mouse twitch its tiny whiskers. Eagles have five times more sensory cells in their eyes compared to humans, which allows them to see small details. They have two "screens" on their retina (people have just one) which improves clarity in their vision. Finally, while people see three different colors (blue, red and yellow), eagles see five different colors allowing them to pick out camouflaging animals with ease.

SYMBOL Eagles of all kinds have been symbols of strength and freedom for thousands of years. The Roman military placed the Golden Eagle on their official flag nearly three thousand years ago. It is currently the national symbol of Mexico, in the same way that the Bald Eagle is the national symbol of the U.S.A.

family field guide

TALONS

Eagles use their talons to catch and kill their prey. Their toe muscles are able to squeeze two times tighter than human jaw muscles and the talons are as sharp as knives. They are able to carry up to 8 pounds in flight, slightly less than the weight of an average-sized raccoon.

SOARING

Golden Eagles are soaring birds. They require large, open areas and upward moving wind currents. At soaring altitudes of 80 feet above the ground, eagles can see up to two miles in all directions. Their good vision and effortless soaring allow them to hunt a five square mile area in several minutes.

HUGE RANGE

Golden Eagles live in more areas than any other eagle. Their range includes North America, northern Africa, Europe and Asia. They can survive on any continent where mountainous terrain creates windy updrafts and where they can soar in wide open areas.

Prey Golden Eagles catch their prey, then carry it back to a feeding perch where they eat.

Talons Like all *raptors*, Golden Eagles use talons to catch and hold their prey.

Goose
(Canada Goose)

PLACE PLACE SIZE

FOOD NEST

MIGRATION MIGRATION

CLASSIFICATION

SCIENTIFIC NAME
Branta canadensis

BIRD FAMILY
Duck, Goose and Swan family

ROCKY MOUNTAIN RELATIVES
All duck species

HABITAT

NEST
Cup-shaped nest built on the ground near water; placed below tall grasses, shrubs or on islands hidden from predators.

FOOD
Grasses, seeds, water plants, roots, algae.

MIGRATION
Varies from no migration to elevational migrations to longer migrations within the southwestern states; some geese migrate to Colorado in winter.

LOYALTY Canada Geese mate for life. Pairs migrate together, returning to the same nesting sites each spring where they nest on islands or in shallow depressions near water. The female sits on the eggs while the male warns off intruders by chasing, hissing and slapping his wings violently. Do not approach nests, as males are aggressive! Newborn *goslings* are able to swim within 24 hours after birth, but they do not mate until their third year.

PROTECTED SPECIES In the early 1900s, Canada Geese were nearly hunted to extinction. The government stocked new populations of geese and enforced seasonal hunting laws in an effort to improve their population. Canada Geese are so abundant today that their droppings litter flocking grounds and they often eat farmers' crops. Nonetheless, these birds are protected and cannot be harmed except by licensed hunters during hunting season.

THEY'RE EVERYWHERE Canada Geese live in city parks and golf courses, and near water sources in grasslands, deserts, canyons and mountains. They require open water for food and protection. Canada Geese are herbivores, eating algae and other water plants as well as grasses, corn, oats and other seed producing plants. They feed on land throughout the day, then sleep on the water where they are safe from predators at night.

family field guide

DOWN WITH THAT?

Geese and other water birds produce soft feathers called *down*. These feathers are small, soft and provide warmth. Because of their softness and warmth, down feathers are a favorite material in jackets, pillows and comforters. Most of the world's down feathers are produced in China and Taiwan.

NECK

The long neck is used to reach water plants from the bottom of shallow lakes and ponds. It is also used in their noisy mating displays in which male geese swing their necks from side to side to attract a female mate.

FEET

Webbed feet allow this bird to swim rapidly in open water.

V-FORMATION

Flocks of flying geese are common fall observations. The flocks are easy to identify by their V-formation, with the first bird, always a female, guiding the flock and working hard to break through the wind. The following birds require less effort as they use air waves created by the lead bird to create lift which allows easier flight. The birds change positions within the formation, sharing the work load and minimizing exhaustion.

V-Formation Canada Geese fly in a V-formation for more efficient migrations.

Nesting Ground nests are vulnerable to predators so geese are aggressive and protective.

Gray Jay
(Canada Jay, Camp Robber)

 PLACE

 PLACE

 PLACE

 SIZE

 FOOD

NEST

MIGRATION

John Rushenberg

CLASSIFICATION

SCIENTIFIC NAME
Parisoreous canadensis

BIRD FAMILY
Raven, Magpie and Jay family

ROCKY MOUNTAIN RELATIVES
Raven, Crow, Clark's Nutcracker, Steller's Jay, Scrub Jay, Pinyon Jay

HABITAT

NEST
Cup-shaped nest in evergreen tree; lined with feathers, animal hair and lichen for softness and warmth.

FOOD
Insects, spiders, berries, seeds, bird eggs, dead animals and hand-outs.

MIGRATION
None.

WATCH, DON'T FEED Close encounters with wildlife create lasting memories. Animals that nag and bully people for food, however, create uncomfortable, and sometimes dangerous, encounters. Feeding these birds, and any type of wildlife, *habituates* them to humans; they begin to expect and depend on people for food. Human food is not healthy for birds and pesky, begging animals become a nuisance to people.

WINTER FEED Gray Jays live in high-mountain evergreen forests where food is in short supply six months of each year. In winter, Gray Jays eat food which they collected and stored in the fall. Before snow falls, the birds collect small bundles of seeds, berries or beef jerky, then coat the food in sticky saliva. The saliva glues the food together in a bundle that sticks into tree cracks and other tiny hiding places. This packaging behavior provides them with a healthy winter food supply.

COSTS OF MIGRATION Gray Jays live twice as long as many birds their size, partly because they do not migrate. Long migrations require huge amounts of energy and provide encounters with dangerous obstacles including bad weather, power lines and cars, to name a few. Most songbirds do not survive more than 4-5 years because of the energy requirements and dangers of migration, but Gray Jays can live as long as ten years.

family field guide

HIDDEN NESTS

Gray Jays find their mates in the fall, remain together through winter, then lay their eggs in early spring. Snow still covers the ground in their nesting sites while pine martens, pine squirrels, ravens, crows, raccoons and porcupines are still surviving on limited food sources. Gray Jay nests are tucked in high evergreen branches in an effort to remain hidden from these forest predators.

CAMP ROBBER

This bird is not recognizable by any brilliant colors or features, but mostly by its behavior. Gray Jays, also called Camp Robbers, are not afraid to approach people in hopes of receiving handouts. The simple act of sitting down and opening a backpack is an invitation for a Gray Jay to perch on a nearby branch.

WHY WINTER?

While many people wonder why Gray Jays choose to live in a cold winter environment, few realize that summer is their most vulnerable season. Jays have plenty of winter food (stored food), warmth (feathers) and protection (evergreen trees), but in summer, forest hawks return and feed heavily on Gray Jay populations.

bitat Gray Jays hide under the cover of green trees throughout the year.

Don't Feed No matter how much they beg, please don't feed these curious scavengers.

family field guide

Great Blue Heron

PLACE

PLACE

SIZE

FOOD

NEST

MIGRATION

CLASSIFICATION

SCIENTIFIC NAME
Ardea herodias

BIRD FAMILY
Heron family

ROCKY MOUNTAIN RELATIVES
Night Heron

HABITAT

NEST
Large colonies of nests called *heronries* are built in tall, sturdy trees near water.

FOOD
Mostly fish; also frogs, salamanders, lizards and small mammals.

MIGRATION
Short migrations to lower elevations within the southwestern United States.

SILENT PREDATOR Great Blue Herons eat fish. They stand like statues in shallow water staring toward their feet. From a fish's point of view, Heron legs look like sturdy yellow grasses growing from the river bottom. Passing fish swim unsuspectingly within inches of the camouflaged legs before the Heron catapults its long neck into the water, catching its prey in its long beak. It patiently holds the fish until it stops wiggling, then tosses it into the air, catching it head-first before swallowing it whole.

AUDUBON SOCIETY Long, colorful feathers decorate the head, neck and tail of the Great Blue Heron. In the late 1800s these feathers were used as decorations for elegant hats. Just as beavers were nearly hunted to extinction because their fur was used for hat making, Great Blue Herons were also on the brink of extinction for fashion's sake. In 1896, an upper class woman named Augustus Hemenway was angered by the killing of birds for their feathers. She started an organization called the Massachusettes Audubon Society. Today, 120 years later, her organization has grown to be called the National Audubon Society and remains a leading conservation organization.

HUGE WINGS Great Blue Herons have a wingspan similar to that of Golden Eagles and Turkey Vultures but Herons are easy to identify by their long legs which extend behind them in flight.

family field guide

COMMUNITY LIVING

Great Blue Herons live in community nests called *heronries* along rivers, streams, lakes and ponds in most every state in America. Heronries may include several nests or several dozen nests, all built in the same tree or group of trees. A single tree may act as an apartment complex for a dozen or more birds which are constantly taking off, landing, feeding, and chatting throughout the day. Heronries provide fun bird watching, but please use binoculars and don't wander too close. Herons return each year to the same heronry as long as they are not commonly disturbed.

BIG FISH

Dippers, Kingfishers, Osprey and Great Blue Herons all hunt for fish, but they do not compete for the same fish. Dippers may eat finger-sized fish, Kingfishers feed on hand-sized fish, Osprey eat full-grown fish from the middle of lakes or rivers and Herons eat full-grown fish, usually from the edges of lakes or rivers. These different feeding habits allow many fish eaters to share the same waterways.

BEAK

A Heron's beak is a hunting tool. Though it forms a sharp point, it is not used for spearing. The sharpest part of the beak is the inside edge which is razor-sharp and is lined with tiny slivers which slant backward to prevent slippery fish from wiggling out of its grasp.

Water Hunter Long legs allow the Great Blue Heron to stand quietly in shallow water.

Heronry Communities of many nests are built in large trees and may house several dozen birds.

Grouse
(Blue Grouse, Dusky Grouse)

PLACE   PLACE   SIZE

FOOD   FOOD

NEST MIGRATION

CLASSIFICATION

SCIENTIFIC NAME
Dendragapus obscurus

BIRD FAMILY
Grouse and Turkey family

ROCKY MOUNTAIN RELATIVES
Wild Turkey, White-tailed Ptarmigan

HABITAT

NEST
Grassy nests on the ground beneath fallen trees or thick shrubs.

FOOD
Insects, whortleberry, aspen leaves, dandelions, clover, strawberries, elderberries, raspberries, evergreen needles.

MIGRATION
Montane and subalpine forests in summer; lower montane forests in winter.

National Park Service

MOUNTAIN CHICKEN Blue Grouse live mostly on the ground grazing on plants, berries, seeds and insects. Their grazing lifestyle affords them the nickname Mountain Chicken. They rely more on camouflage for protection than on flight. When startled by passing hikers or the threat of predators, Blue Grouse erupt from the ground with loud and startling wing beats to roost in nearby treetops. Similar to chickens, they typically fly downhill and rarely fly more than a hundred yards at a time.

GROWING UP Females make their nests by scraping a clearing of dirt beneath a fallen tree or under a well-protected thicket. The nest is lined with dead twigs, grasses and pine needles. After 3-4 weeks of *incubation*, the eggs hatch. Within 24 hours, the babies learn to feed themselves and the family abandons the nest and begins to wander together through the forest in the same way that a family of ducks swims together in a lake.

SHORT MIGRATION Adult Blue Grouse live in douglas fir and lodgepole pine forests in winter. During mating season they move to open aspen forests at the edge of sage flats and lowland shrubs. Females stay in the lower forests to raise their young, while males move to upper montane and subalpine forests through late summer.

family field guide

MATING DANCE

The Grouse and Turkey family are known for exotic mating displays which occur in April. Male Blue Grouse have orange "eye brows" and skin patches on the sides of their neck. In display, they puff their neck with air, exposing the bright neck patches and flare their tail feathers like a Peacock. Dressed in their mating colors, they strut in circles, beat their wings and call to all females within a half-mile. Eleven months of the year, these birds are secretive, silent and hidden on the ground, then, for one month in spring, they promote their identity to all who can hear. During this month, males accept as many mates as possible but do not build a nest, raise the babies or remain with any female for even a single day.

MOUNTAIN BLUEBERRY

In summer, Blue Grouse most commonly live in forests covered by Grouse Whortleberry (*Vaccinium scoparium*). This ground-cover plant grows less than a foot tall beneath evergreen forests and produces tiny berries in late summer. Grouse eat both the leaves and the berries.

HUNTED

Blue Grouse are a "small game species" and are hunted from September through November. Hunters must have a permit to legally kill grouse or any other small game.

Mating Males perform a spring display to attract their female mates.

Camouflage Blue Grouse depend more on camouflage than on flight for protection.

Hummingbird
(Broad-tailed Hummingbird)

PLACE	PLACE	PLACE

SIZE	FOOD	FOOD

NEST	MIGRATION

National Park Service

CLASSIFICATION

SCIENTIFIC NAME
Selasphorus platycercus

BIRD FAMILY
Hummingbird family

ROCKY MOUNTAIN RELATIVES
Rufous Hummingbird

HABITAT

NEST
Cup-shaped nests made from lichen, leaves, shredded bark, plant fibers, hairs, spider silk.

FOOD
Mostly flower nectar; also insects, spiders and tree sap from Sapsucker wells.

MIGRATION
Migration to Mexico starts in mid-August.

COLORS Male Broad-tailed Hummingbirds have a bright red patch under their chins called a *gorget*. The bright color, however, is only visible when the bird is facing directly toward the observer because the gorget feathers are not actually red. Instead, the tiny feathers are arranged at angles that reflect red light.

HOVERING Hummingbirds are able to flap their wings in a way that allows them to fly forward, backward, sideways or to hover in one place. Similar to bumble bees, this unique flying ability allows them to fly from flower to flower without ever landing on a perch. When hovering, hummingbirds hold their body upright with their wings flapping in a figure-eight pattern which pushes wind up, down and to each side so fast that they remain in one place.

FAST BIRD Everything about hummingbirds is fast. They flap their wings faster than any other birds, 3,000-5,000 wing beats per minute during normal flight. Their heart beats up to 1,250 times per minute and they are able to fly up to 40 miles per hour during their long migration south. By comparison, a person can flap its arms 160 times per minute with a heart rate of 120 beats per minute. An olympic runner can reach top speeds of 20 miles per hour. In cold weather, however, when hummingbirds need to conserve energy, they can drop their heart rate to 50 beats per minute, slower than a human's resting rate.

family field guide

NESTING

If a female's eggs hatch successfully in the spring, she will often return the next year to rebuild her nest in the same location. Her sense of direction is so sharp that females often nest in the same tree, on the same branch and sometimes use the previous year's nesting material for the new nest!

WHISTLE

Male Broad-tailed Hummingbirds are often heard before they are seen. The longest feathers on their wings are angled in a way that causes the wind to whistle as it passes through the flight feathers. The whistling sound is used to show aggression towards intruders and allows them to better defend their territories. Only the males have these whistling wings.

MIGRATION

These tiny birds fly up to 400 miles each fall to mountains in Mexico and Guatemala, then return back to the Rocky Mountains each spring! This bird, which weighs less than a quarter, negotiates storms and strong winds with very strong flight muscles.

Nest Hummingbirds use lichen, spider webs, pine cone scales and other small materials for nests.

Insects Hummingbirds eat insects as well as flower nectar.

Kingfisher
(Belted Kingfisher)

PLACE

PLACE

SIZE

FOOD

NEST

MIGRATION
MIGRATION

C. Schlawe   US Fish and Wildlife Service

CLASSIFICATION

SCIENTIFIC NAME
Megaceryle alcyon

BIRD FAMILY
Kingfisher family

ROCKY MOUNTAIN RELATIVES
None

HABITAT

NEST
Burrows a long hole deep into sandy cliff walls; usually near water.

FOOD
Mostly small fish (under 6" long); also crayfish, lizards, frogs, salamanders, snakes, insects, young birds, mice and dried berries.

MIGRATION
Some remain all winter; others migrate to lower elevations within the southern United States.

RIPARIAN HUNTER Belted Kingfishers depend mostly on small fish for food. They perch on branches or hover above open water looking through the clear surface for small fish, usually less than six inches long. Once they spy their prey, they dive beak first into the water, open their mouth, snatch the shallow-swimming fish, then carry it back to their perch. They throw the fish in the air, catch it sideways in their beak, then smack the fish's head against a tree branch. Next, they throw the fish in the air a second time, catch it head-first, then swallow it whole. They must eat the fish head-first so that the scales do not get caught in their throat. When water is cloudy, they hunt for different kinds of food.

LEARNING As soon as young birds can fly, they begin learning how to hunt. Adult birds catch small fish, kill them and drop them in the water for the young birds to retrieve. Babies sometimes drown in their first attempts to dive into the water. Adults feed the young birds for several weeks while they are learning to hunt, but within weeks they are able to catch enough food to survive on their own.

RELATIVES The Belted Kingfisher is common throughout North America, but is the only member of the colorful and varied Kingfisher family on this continent (except for a few Ringed and Green Kingfishers in southern Texas).

family field guide

BEAK

The Kingfisher beak is long enough to dip below the water to catch shallow-swimming fish. Small slits are angled backward so that slippery fish cannot slide out of their grasp. In flight, Kingfishers rise with each wingbeat, then fall between beats because of their large, heavy beak.

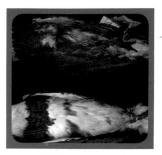

MALES AND FEMALES

The Belted Kingfisher is one of few species where the female (top) is more colorful than the male (bottom). Their name comes from the "belt" around the male's breast.

NEST

Kingfishers use their beaks to burrow into muddy or sandy cliff walls. They dig deep into the soft wall, then create a small nesting chamber at the end. They do not pad their nest with feathers, grasses or any soft material, simply laying their eggs on the dirt. This deep burrow protects them from predators, but is very difficult to clean. Kingfisher nests are often littered with dried food remains and poop. For this resason, each nest is only used for one season before it is abandoned.

Fish Eater Even small fish provide big meals for this small carnivore.

Nest Kingfishers burrow into soft cliffs making a hole the size of a softball.

Magpie
(Black-billed Magpie)

FOOD   NEST

MIGRATION   MIGRATION

National Park Service

CLASSIFICATION

SCIENTIFIC NAME
Pica hudsonia

BIRD FAMILY
Raven, Jay and Magpie family

ROCKY MOUNTAIN RELATIVES
Raven, Crow, Gray Jay, Clark's Nutcracker, Stellar's Jay, Scrub Jay, Pinyon Jay

HABITAT

NEST
Globe-shaped nest the size of a basketball is made of sticks.

FOOD
Insects, seeds, berries, nuts, dead animals, small mammals, baby birds and eggs; garbage in winter.

MIGRATION
Some move to lower elevations within Colorado; many remain in the mountains through winter.

NAME The name Magpie refers both to this bird's appearance and its behavior. The first half of their name refers to the maggots (baby flies) which live in the dead animals they eat. The last part of their name comes from the old word "piebald" which means white, and refers to the white wing and belly feathers. The two words, maggots and piebald, are shortened, then combined to make the name Magpie.

NEIGHBORLY Magpies are one of the easiest birds to observe in the Rocky Mountain region because they live comfortably among human populations and they are large, unique and easy to identify. Magpies roost on neighborhood fence posts, eat from backyard fruit trees, stand on garbage cans by the curb and are common suburban visitors. Their constant presence inspires opinions among many observers. Some love their beautiful colors, some dislike their scavenging ways, but many, having seen them so regularly in their daily routines, pay little attention to this uniquely common resident.

NOISE MAKER As with all members of the Jay family, the Magpie is a noisy bird. Its loud call is easy to identify once it has been heard enough times. Given the opportunity you might also hear a delightful array of chattering, chirping, crackling and cackling, all of which have different meanings in this bird's complex communication system.

family field guide

WESTERN BIRD

Magpies only live west of the Mississippi River. Visitors from the eastern half of the country observing this bird for the first time often consider the Magpie as one of the most ornate and beautiful of western birds.

FEATHERS

At first glance, Magpie feathers are black and white. However, when the sun shines right, the wing and tail feathers shine with hints of green, blue, purple and bronze.

OPPORTUNISTS

Magpies are *opportunists* which means that they eat any food that is available. They mostly eat insects, seeds, nuts and berries in spring and summer, but in winter, when food is in short supply, they eat dead animals, garbage and anything they can find.

NESTS

Magpies require over a month to build a nest from scratch A large bundle of sticks is woven together in a tangle of tree branches, then a soft grassy nest is placed in its center. Finally, a dome of branches is laced over the top of the nest, leaving only a small entryway on the side, which is safe from predators. Magpies commonly repair old nests each season, but owls and hawks often take over previous year's nests, forcing the Magpie pair to rebuild.

Scavenger Magpies will eat almost anything and depend greatly on dead animals in winter.

Tail The obvious long tail is used for balance and direction in flight.

family field guide

Mallard

PLACE

PLACE

SIZE

FOOD

NEST

MIGRATION

MIGRATION

CLASSIFICATION

SCIENTIFIC NAME
Anas platyrhynchos

BIRD FAMILY
Duck, Goose and Swan family

ROCKY MOUNTAIN RELATIVES
Canada Goose and all duck species

HABITAT

NEST
Cup-shaped nest hidden on the ground near shallow water.

FOOD
Water plants, seeds and grasses, aquatic insects and *mollusks*.

MIGRATION
Some remain in the mountains through winter, others migrate to lower elevations within the southwestern states.

DABBLERS Mallards belong to a group of ducks called *dabbling* ducks. Dabbling ducks feed from the surface of the water and are unable to dive for food. While feeding, their tails point straight up in the air as their bills reach to the lake bottom. Mallards can only feed in shallow lakes and ponds where they can reach food without diving.

COLD FEET A thin layer of skin grows between the front three toes of all ducks. These webbed feet allow ducks to swim easily in water. This thin skin looks as if it would freeze in cold temperatures. The blood vessels in the skin, however, are arranged in a way that keeps their feet warm. As blood pumps from the heart and passes through veins, the blood is warm. In duck feet, veins are placed nearly in contact with arteries so that the warm blood in the veins warms the blood in the arteries allowing the feet to stay a constant temperature.

WATERPROOFING Birds that live in water need to waterproof their feathers to improve flotation and increase warmth in cold weather. When they clean themselves, they poke their beak into an oil gland located near their tail, then spread the oil through their feathers. The oily surface of the feathers causes water to slide off the feathers without leaking into their skin. Mallards spend several hours every day waterproofing their feathers.

family field guide

MOLTING

Each year, sometimes several times each year, old worn-out feathers fall out and new, healthy feathers grow in their place. This process, called *molting*, happens to all bird species and takes several weeks. In mid-summer, Mallards molt their flight feathers and are unable to fly. During these flightless weeks, males grow new head feathers which are brown so they look very similar to females. This camouflaged appearance adds protection during these vulnerable weeks before green feathers grow again.

WHISTLING WINGS

In flight, Mallards are easy to identify from other ducks by the whistling sound made by their wings. Other ducks fly much more quietly.

EARLY PAIRING

Unlike many birds which attract mates in early spring, male and female Mallards choose their mates in the fall. The pair migrates together in winter, if they migrate at all, then return to their breeding place in spring. While Canada Geese are performing their mating displays in April and May, Mallards have already established their mates.

BOYS AND GIRLS

Male Mallards are called *drakes* and females are called *hens*. The bright green head feathers of the drakes attract females, while the brown color of the hens is used as camouflage while sitting on their eggs.

Molt In mid-summer males' heads (above) loose their green color while they are *molting*.

Drakes and Hens Male Mallards (right) are colorful while females (left) are camouflaged.

Meadowlark
(Western Meadowlark)

John & Karen Hollingsworth   US Fish and Wildlife Service

CLASSIFICATION

SCIENTIFIC NAME
Sturnella neglecta

BIRD FAMILY
Blackbirds, Meadowlarks and Orioles

ROCKY MOUNTAIN RELATIVES
Red-winged Blackbird, Common Grackle, Yellow-headed Blackbird, Brown-headed Cowbird, Brewer's Blackbird

HABITAT

NEST
Cup-shaped depressions are dug in the ground beneath tall grasses.

FOOD
Mostly caterpillars, grasshoppers and other insects and grass seeds.

MIGRATION
Migrate to lower elevation grasslands in the western United States.

SURVIVAL OF THE FITTEST Male Meadowlarks arrive in early spring to their breeding grounds and work hard to establish their territories. Males may clasp their feet together and peck one another with their long pointed beaks to determine the most powerful male in the area. Once the strongest Meadowlark has been identified, he perches throughout the day on fence posts or tall branches and sings his fluted song to warn off other males.

MATING DISPLAY After the males have had several weeks to establish their territories, the females arrive to the breeding grounds. While males are maintaining their territories, the females admire the colorful singers. When a male spots an admiring female, he is likely to sing his song repeatedly while puffing up his bright yellow chest and cheeks. Next, he flaps his wings over his head several times and hops up and down on his perch.

GROUND NESTING Meadowlarks are uniquely colorful *and* camouflaged. Their bright colored breast allows easy identification, but their streaked back allows them to sit unnoticed on a nest. The camouflaged feathers are especially important for the females who build their dome-covered nests on the ground where coyotes, foxes, bobcats and other predators wander.

GAPING

Meadowlarks have adapted a unique behavior called *gaping* which allows them to search for caterpillars, grasshoppers and other bugs hiding in tall and tangled grasses. While some carnivores have developed muscles which *close* their jaws with incredible strength, Meadowlarks have developed muscles which allow them to *open* their jaws with equal strength. These insect eaters poke their long, slender beaks into a tangle of overgrown grasses, then use their strong beak muscles to pry open the tangled mess of grasses. As they pry apart the grassy hiding place, their eyes roll forward allowing them to look directly into the narrow opening where tiny bugs are hiding.

TWO BROODS

Males allow two mates into their territory, each of which produces two sets of eggs each summer. Each set, or *brood*, produces 3-6 babies, so male meadowlarks can produce 20 or more babies in a summer!

CALL OF THE WILD

Meadowlarks are best known by their call. Though impossible to describe on paper, the Western Meadowlark is most easily identified by its flute-like series of notes played out over grasslands and open pastures.

Nest These ground nests are usually covered with a grassy roof and are very hard to see.

Colors The yellow breast attracts a mate and the brown back camouflages against tall grasses.

Mountain Bluebird

PLACE

PLACE

SIZE

FOOD

NEST

MIGRATION

National Park Service

CLASSIFICATION

SCIENTIFIC NAME
Sialia currucoides

BIRD FAMILY
Thrush family

ROCKY MOUNTAIN RELATIVES
American Robin, Hermit Thrush and Swainson's Thrush

HABITAT

NEST
Abandoned woodpecker holes or cracks in rocks.

FOOD
Insects in flight and on the ground in summer; dried berries in winter.

MIGRATION
To lower elevation grasslands within the Southwestern United States.

INSECTIVORE Mountain Bluebirds are fun to watch while they are hunting. These birds eat insects which they find in open meadows where viewing is easy. When hunting in open meadows with few perches, Mountain Bluebirds can hover for 30 seconds or more, then fly to another spot and hover again and again until they locate food. Once they spot their prey, they drop quickly to grab it. When fence posts or tree limbs, are present, they perch patiently until flying insects pass nearby, then leap out several feet, grab the bug in mid-flight and return to the perch to eat their feast. This hunting strategy is called *hawking*.

CAVITY NESTING Mountain Bluebirds nest in tree cavities, but unlike woodpeckers, they are not able to build their own. Instead, they use abandoned woodpecker holes or naturally rotted cavities, usually in dead trees. Burned forests provide excellent nesting grounds for Mountain Bluebirds because natural cavities occur commonly in the dead and rotting tree trunks.

COLOR Male Mountain Bluebirds are bright blue while females are dull blue with a gray belly. Surprisingly, Mountain Bluebird feathers do not contain blue-colored cells (*pigments*). The blue feathers of most birds are created by the arrangement of feathers which reflect blue waves of light rather than by cells which contain a blue color.

family field guide

NEST BOXES

Mountain Bluebirds commonly nest in tree trunks that have been burned. In the mid-1900s, the number and size of forest fires was heavily controlled by forest managers. Many scientists believe that this method of managing forest fires limited the number of nesting sites for Mountain Bluebirds, causing a decline in their population. Recently, people have been encouraged to place bluebird nesting boxes on fence posts surrounding pastures, meadows and open forests. Scientists estimate that over half of all Mountain Bluebirds today build nests in nesting boxes provided by thoughtful land owners.

BLUE FEATHERS

Most blue-colored feathers are created by blue waves of light which reflect off of the feathers. To prove this theory, look at a blue-colored feather in a dim room with a light placed behind the feather. If it appears blue, the feather contains blue-colored cells. If it appears dull brown, the blue color is created by the reflection of blue-colored light waves, but only when light hits the *top* of the feather.

STATE BIRD

The Mountain Bluebird is the state bird of Idaho and Nevada.

Nest Mountain Bluebirds use old woodpecker holes or natural cavities for nesting.

Female Female Mountain Bluebirds have a gray back, light breast and blue tail and flight feathers.

family field guide

Nuthatch
(White-breasted Nuthatch)

PLACE	PLACE	SIZE

SUMMER	WINTER

NEST	MIGRATION

National Park Service

CLASSIFICATION

SCIENTIFIC NAME
Sitta carolinensis

BIRD FAMILY
Nuthatch family

ROCKY MOUNTAIN RELATIVES
Red-breasted Nuthatch

HABITAT

NEST
A cup-shaped nest is built inside abandoned woodpecker holes.

FOOD
Insects including ants, termites, beetles, caterpillars and spiders; dried berries and seeds in winter.

MIGRATION
None

HATCHING *Hatch* is an old word that describes a hammering technique (think of the word "hatchet"). In summer, Nuthatches eat insects and spiders which they collect from tiny cracks and crevices in tree bark, but their name originates from their seed-eating behavior which increases in winter. After collecting a seed, some animals must crack open the shell before eating the nut inside (think of eating a sunflower seed). Nuthatches crack shells by lodging seeds tightly into small cracks in tree bark, then they hammer the shell with their beak to get to the nut inside.

WINTER FLOCKS In summer, Nuthatches defend a small territory where they nest and forage for food. In winter, however, food is less common so the birds use a large area. During this time, they join flocks of chickadees and titmice in their search for food. Flocking helps protect the birds from predators because more birds have more eyes to watch for predators. In this way each bird can focus more attention on finding food than on watching for danger.

BIRD FEEDERS In winter, when insects and spiders are less abundant, Nuthatches commonly feed at bird feeders. This is the best time to observe them collecting seeds and nuts from the feeder and "hatching" them in nearby tree branches.

family field guide

BILL SWEEPING

Nuthatches nest in abandoned woodpecker holes or natural tree cavities, but occasionally dig out their own cavities in soft or rotten trees. After building a small nest of bark, grasses and feathers within the cavity, Nuthatches have been observed "sweeping" the cavity entrance with animal fur, grasses or insect guts. Scientists believe that this behavior, called "bill sweeping," Is an attempt to mask their odor so that predators do not smell them.

UP AND DOWN

A Nuthatch's ability to walk up and down vertical tree trunks is unique. Woodpeckers commonly walk up tree trunks in search of hiding insects, but walking down is unique to the Nuthatches.

HABITAT

Nuthatches prefer to nest and feed in evergreen trees because they can hide among the dense branches. However, they are most easily observed foraging in large deciduous trees, like Cottonwoods, where they are exposed on the wide tree trunks.

Relative The Red-breasted Nuthatch has a dark stripe through its eye. Both species nest in holes.

Tree Walker Unlike woodpeckers, Nuthatches walk up *and* down tree trunks in search of insects.

Osprey

PLACE

PLACE

SIZE

FOOD

NEST

MIGRATION

CLASSIFICATION

SCIENTIFIC NAME
Pandion haliaetus

BIRD FAMILY
Osprey family

ROCKY MOUNTAIN RELATIVES
None

HABITAT

NEST
Obvious cup-shaped nests placed in treetops or other platforms near water.

FOOD
Fish

MIGRATION
Migrate to lower elevations within the southern United States.

FISH FEEDER Osprey are fish-eating specialists; 99% of their diet is fish! This characteristic is enough to classify them in their own family unique from hawks or eagles. They soar 30-100 feet above water, locate shallow swimming fish, hover briefly, then dive in for the kill. As they approach the water, they lower their legs, grab the fish and carry it back to their perch where it is eaten.

NESTING Osprey always nest near water. The nests, a cup-shaped bundle of large sticks, are built in forks of large trees, on rocky outcrops and on man-made structures including telephone poles, signs posts and platforms. Scientists and conservation organizations have built thousands of platforms in lakes and rivers around the country to increase quality Osprey nesting habitat. These raptors consistently use the man-made nesting platforms and are not disturbed by large amounts of human activity.

HUGE RANGE Osprey live on every continent except Antarctica. They live along rivers, lakes, wetlands and oceans feeding on all varieties of freshwater and saltwater fish. They typically catch fish weighing less than two pounds. Occasionally, Osprey try to catch larger fish which are strong enough to drag a raptor under water! If the talons get caught in such a large, strong fish, the Osprey may be dragged under water where it can drown.

family field guide

POPULATION RECOVERY

Between 1950 and 1972, Osprey populations dropped rapidly throughout the United States. Scientists suggested that a commonly used chemical called DDT, which was sprayed from airplanes onto farmers' crops, landed in lakes, creeks and rivers. As a result, plants and insects in and near the water absorbed the poison, then the fish became poisoned and the fish-eating carnivores absorbed the highest levels of DDT. Today, Osprey populations are healthy and stable following the 1972 ban on DDT.

SYMBOL

Osprey are admired by many as an impressive flier and a skilled hunter. It is the *provincial* bird of Nova Scotia, Canada and the official mascot of several universities in the United States. A less commonly used name for the Osprey is a Seahawk, the mascot for the Seattle-based football team.

STICKY FEET

Osprey have tiny bumps on the bottoms of their feet, each of which has a small hook on it. These barbed pads act like Velcro against slippery fish scales and help prevent the squirmy fish from slipping out of their grasp.

National Park Service

Fish Eater Osprey feed almost entirely on fish which they catch with their talons.

Lee Karney US Fish and Wildlife Service

In Flight Osprey have white bodies, angled wings and fly most of the time near water.

family field guide

Owl
(Great-horned Owl)

SIZE   **FOOD**

NEST   **MIGRATION**

National Park Service

CLASSIFICATION

SCIENTIFIC NAME
Bubo virginianus

BIRD FAMILY
Typical owl family

ROCKY MOUNTAIN RELATIVES
Western Screech Owl, Boreal Owl, Northern Saw-whet Owl, Northern Pygmy Owl

HABITAT

NEST
Use abandoned magpie, eagle, hawk or heron nests in sturdy treetops.

FOOD
Mostly small mammals including voles, deer mice, rabbits and hares; also hawk and heron nestlings, domestic cats, lizards and other small animals.

MIGRATION
None

DIET Scientists have identified over 250 different prey species eaten by Great-horned Owls worldwide. This list includes frogs, fish and salamanders; mice, moles and voles; centipedes, grasshoppers and worms; dogs, cats and chickens; skunks, porcupines and raccoons; snakes, lizards and many more. They are able to catch animals 2-3 times their size which they carry back to their perch and eat in small pieces. More commonly, they eat small animals which they can swallow whole. Owls are the only predator which are not affected by a skunk's offensive odor because they do not have a sense of smell!

SILENT HUNTER Owls depend on silent flight to surprise their prey. Their lead flight feather is fringed which quiets the wind as it passes over the wing. These feathers allow all Owl species to flap their wings silently. By comparison, a flapping Raven wing stirs up the air causing it to pass loudly through and around the straight, stiff flight feathers!

RANGE Great-horned Owls live in every state, Canada, Mexico and throughout Central America. They roost in natural tree cavities and put very little effort into creating much of a nest. During breeding season, they use abandoned hawk, raven, heron or crow nests. While the species has a large range, individual birds rarely move more than fifty miles from the site where they were born.

family field guide

HORNS

These large owls are named for the horn-like feathers which stick up from their head. These feathers are neither horns nor ears. Some scientists think that they are used to communicate with other owls and that they help the owls' shape to camouflage against tree branches.

NECK

While owls' eyes are huge and are adapted to night vision, they cannot move from side-to-side. If an owl wants to see an object located outside of its field of vision, it moves its head rather than its eyes. As a result, owls have twice as many vertebrae in their necks as humans, allowing them to turn their heads 270 degrees. They cannot turn their heads all the way around, but they can look directly backward and even a bit beyond.

EARS

Owls use sound more than sight for locating prey. Their round face absorbs sound waves, tiny feathers around their face act like whiskers that are sensitive to sound waves, and one ear opens slightly higher up the head than the other. This *asymmetrical* placement allows the bird to turn its head side-to-side until the sound is equal in both ears, then to tilt its head up and down until the sound is equal in both ears. At this point, the owl has found the exact location of its prey, or a possible predator, without ever using its eyes!

FEATHERED FEET

Unlike most birds of prey, owl feet are feathered which allows them to stay warm during cold winter months.

Big Eyes Owls have good hearing and night vision. Both are important for *nocturnal* hunting.

Nests Owls use abandoned nests from other birds rather than building their own.

family field guide

Ptarmigan
(White-tailed Ptarmigan)

PLACE

SIZE

FOOD

NEST

MIGRATION

John Rushenberg

CLASSIFICATION

SCIENTIFIC NAME
Lagopus leucurus

BIRD FAMILY
Grouse and Turkey family

ROCKY MOUNTAIN RELATIVES
Blue Grouse and Wild Turkey

HABITAT

NEST
Ground nests placed below tall grasses or thick willows; often near streams.

FOOD
Willow leaves and buds, flowers, berries; evergreen needles and lichen in winter.

MIGRATION
Females move down into evergreen forests while males move to the edge of treeline.

WINTER BIRD Ptarmigan are built to survive deep snow, cold temperatures and long winters. Stiff feathers cover their feet providing warmth and snowshoe-like platforms for walking on the snow. Their round body shape and *downy* feathers hold in warmth and keep out cold. In extreme temperatures and winds, Ptarmigan burrow under the snow for extra protection. No matter the snow depth, evergreen needles are always available as a food source. Because they are able to survive cold temperatures and winter food is always present, Ptarmigan are unique birds that are able to survive high-mountain winters.

CHANGING FEATHERS Like its relatives, the Wild Turkey and the Blue Grouse, Ptarmigan depend more on camouflage than on flight for protection. For this reason, their feathers change color with the seasons. In summer, their streaked brown *plumage* blends with rocks and grasses. After the first fall snow, they begin to grow white feathers, so their bodies are part white and part brown, the same as the hillsides. Once the ground is white with snow, the feathers are all white, too. As the snow begins to melt in spring, brown feathers gradually grow, so the birds again are partly white, partly brown and can camouflage with the partly melted hillsides. As the hillside changes with the seasons, so do the feathers of the Ptarmigan.

family field guide

NEEDLE DIET

Ptarmigan, Grouse and Snowshoe Hare are three of the only animals in the region that eat evergreen needles; most animals cannot digest these waxy "leaves." Ptarmigan have special pouches in their intestines which contain bacteria designed to digest the *cellulose* in evergreen needles. In summer and fall, when they do not eat needles, these pouches shrink and in winter, when needles are an important part of their diet, the pouches expand and the amount of needle-digesting bacteria increases.

ORANGE BROW

Male Ptarmigan have an orange patch of skin above their eyes. This orange skin, the only part of their bodies which does not camouflage with their surroundings, is used to attract females in the spring.

INDICATOR SPECIES

Ptarmigan eat willow buds and leaves in summer. Willows grow along stream beds from the alpine tundra to the lowland shrubs and they often absorb any chemicals which flow in the water. According to the book *Wild At Heart*, a chemical called Cadmium commonly flows out of old mines into the streambeds. If Cadmium flows from the mine into the water, it is absorbed by the willows and eaten by the Ptarmigan, which then get sick. Scientists can study Ptarmigan populations to determine if Cadmium and other chemicals are polluting high mountain streams.

Feet Feathered feet provide warmth and also act like snowshoes when walking on snow.

Camouflage Ptarmigan depend more on camouflage than on flight for protection.

Raven
(Common Raven)

PLACE PLACE PLACE

SIZE FOOD

NEST MIGRATION

National Park Service

CLASSIFICATION

SCIENTIFIC NAME
Corvus corax

BIRD FAMILY
Raven, Magpie and Jay family

ROCKY MOUNTAIN RELATIVES
Magpie, Steller's Jay, Scrub Jay, Pinyon Jay, Clark's Nutcracker, Gray Jay, American Crow

HABITAT

NEST
Large, obvious nests built in tall trees, cliffs or other tall structures.

FOOD
Mostly dead animals; also insects, small rodents, seeds, bird eggs and *nestlings*; garbage in winter.

MIGRATION
None; some move to lower elevations with less snow.

OPPORTUNISTS Ravens are *opportunists* that eat any type of food, whenever it is available. As *scavengers*, they mostly eat dead animals, but also grains and fruits from farmers' fields, small mammals, young birds and bird eggs, amphibians and insects. In winter, when food supplies are limited, they eat from local dumps and garbage cans. Ravens' ability to eat any available food allows them to live in diverse ecosystems throughout the northern hemisphere.

INTELLIGENCE Ravens are one of the most intelligent bird species in the world. Intelligence in this case is defined by their ability to solve problems and to communicate. Ravens in Yellowstone National Park have learned that people store food behind the seats of snowmobiles. The food is secured by a heavy flap of leather or rubber and is fastened by Velcro or other sticky material, but this security system is no match for Raven intelligence. Ravens commonly work in pairs with one bird unleashing the flap and holding it open while the other bird steals the food.

RANGE The Common Raven lives in most every ecosystem in the world, except for tropical rainforests. They live throughout northern Europe and Asia, the Middle East, Northern Africa, North America and Central America as far south as Nicaragua.

family field guide

VOICE

Ravens are very vocal birds and are able to make a wide range of sounds. They use their voices to make alarm calls, comfort calls, chase calls, territorial calls and more. Many scientists believe that they are able to imitate the sounds of other animals or even the human voice, but no scientist has proven this. Ravens also communicate by clicking their beaks, making whistling sounds with their wings and with body language which indicates *dominance* or *submissiveness* with other birds.

RAVENS AND CROWS

Ravens and Crows are easily mistaken for one another. Both birds are solid black, live in similar habitats and have similar behaviors. The best indicator between the two is that Ravens are larger and their tail has a pointed, wedge shape, while Crow tails are rounded. Crows at one time were more common in urban areas and Ravens more common in wild habitats, but as urban areas expand, Crows and Ravens are both common visitors to urban environments.

PROTECTION

Ravens are rarely preyed on by eagles, hawks or owls. Even *nestlings* and eggs are rarely taken by predators. They use their large size and aggressive behavior to protect the nests . When threatened, they call to neighboring Ravens which work together to chase predators up to $1/2$-mile away from the nesting sites.

Flight Feathers The black silhouette shows "fingers" as the flight feathers spread slightly.

Beak The strong, large beak is designed to eat a wide variety of foods.

Red-tailed Hawk

National Park Service

CLASSIFICATION

SCIENTIFIC NAME
Buteo jamaicensis

BIRD FAMILY
Eagle, Hawk and Harrier family

ROCKY MOUNTAIN RELATIVES
Northern Goshawk, Cooper's, Swainson's and Sharp-shinned Hawks, Golden and Bald Eagles

HABITAT

NEST
Cup-shaped nest built of sticks; placed in tall trees or cliff ledges and lined with soft materials.

FOOD
Small to medium-sized rodents, rabbits, hares, birds and snakes.

MIGRATION
To lower elevations with less snow.

COMMON OBSERVATIONS Red-tailed Hawks are large and are the most common member of the *soaring hawk* family which also includes Rough-legged, Ferruginous and Swainson's Hawks. They live in every state, Canada and Mexico, so no matter where you live or travel in North America, it is likely that Red-tailed Hawks live there. Soaring hawks soar on warm rising winds over open fields where they hunt for small mammals. Comparatively, *forest hawks* (Cooper's and Sharp-shinned Hawks and Northern Goshawk) fly quickly through forests and are less obvious to casual observers.

DIFFICULT IDENTIFICATION Red-tailed Hawks are not as easy to identify as one might guess. The tell-tale sign of adult birds is the reddish-brown tail, but young hawks up to two years old have brown tail feathers. Similarly, the red color in the tail feathers varies among adults. Even some adult birds have a tail that is more brown than red.

FALCONRY Falconry is the art of training raptors to fly from a perch, locate and capture wild prey, then return to the perch with food for the trainer. Red-tailed Hawks have been used in falconry for over 2,000 years and are still used in the sport today. Falconry is much less popular today than the peak of its practice in Europe 1,000 years ago.

family field guide

WING SHAPE

Soaring hawks, like the Red-tailed, have broad, flat wings. They commonly hunt over vast open meadows in mid-day when warm air rises, pushes upward on their wings and allows them to soar effortlessly. In contrast, forest hawks, like the Northern Goshawk, have V-shaped wings like a falcon for fast-flying turns in thick forests where they chase and catch songbirds.

VOICE

Red-tailed Hawks have a hoarse, raspy cry. Their cry has been recorded and is used in movies and television commercials to represent the call of any eagle, hawk or other bird of prey.

TALONS AND BEAKS

Like all birds of prey, Red-tailed Hawks use their sharp talons to capture food. Birds do not have teeth, they are much too heavy for flight, so raptors use their beaks to tear off bite-sized chunks for eating.

Hunting Red-tails perch on trees near open meadows where they look for small rodents.

Beak Raptor beaks tear meat into bite-sized pieces. They are not used to catch prey.

Red-winged Blackbird

PLACE

PLACE

SIZE

FOOD

NEST

MIGRATION

US Fish and Wildlife Service

Donna Dewhurst

CLASSIFICATION

SCIENTIFIC NAME
Agelaius phoeniceus

BIRD FAMILY
Meadowlark, Blackbird and Oriole family

ROCKY MOUNTAIN RELATIVES
Brewer's Blackbird, Yellow-headed Blackbird, Brown-headed Cowbird, Grackle, Bullock's Oriole, Western Meadowlark

HABITAT

NEST
Cup-shaped nest woven from grasses marsh plants and mud; attached to the base of living marsh plants.

FOOD
Mainly seeds, but also insects, spiders, worms, snails, crayfish, frogs, lizards, bird eggs, baby birds and berries.

MIGRATION
To lower elevations in Colorado or southern states.

CATTAILS AND PASTURES Red-winged Blackbirds nest in cattail marshes and feed in open fields. The nests are hidden safely among cattails and are suspended just above the ground. Insects in neighboring pastures provide energy-rich summer food.

SPRING SONGS Red-winged Blackbirds are very noisy in spring and early summer. Their song, a melodious *coo-ka-ree*, is unique and obvious in cattail marshes and is used by males to attract mates in spring, then to defend territories in early summer. In July, after the young are born and are flying on their own, the territories are no longer maintained and the marsh becomes quiet. In August, the birds *molt* new feathers before their migration and are flightless for a week or more. During these vulnerable weeks the birds go into hiding before the fall migration.

GROUP LIVING Once breeding season is over, Red-winged Blackbirds live in large flocks. Large populations roost in cattail marshes throughout late summer where they eat insects, seeds and berries. In fall, they migrate south to warmer conditions where thousands of birds roost together in large marshes. These flocks usually include other blackbird species and Starlings. The flocks sleep together at night, then spread out in the day in search of seeds and grains and return at night to the same roosting marsh. Such large flocks can feed heavily on winter crops.

family field guide

RANGE

The Red-winged Blackbird is one of the most common birds in wetlands and agricultural fields. According to Cornell University's Lab of Ornithology, this may be the most abundant of any North American Bird.

MANY MATES

Male Red-winged Blackbirds arrive to their breeding grounds early in the spring. Females arrive up to a month later. A male may attract up to 15 different females to nest within his territory. While the females build nests, the males spend almost all of the daylight hours chasing competing males out of their territory. With so many females under their watch, males cannot keep out all intruders. Up to $1/4$ of all the females within a territory lay eggs fathered by intruder birds.

MALES AND FEMALES

While male Red-winged Blackbirds are easy to identify by their bright red shoulder patches, females are streaked brown and white like sparrows. Any large sparrow-looking bird perched or flying near cattails is likely a female Red-winged Blackbird.

RED WINGS

The males' red shoulder feathers can be flashed as a sign of aggression, in the case of fighting off other males, or attraction, in the case of mating. They can also be hidden if a male is trying to avoid a fight when passing through a neighboring territory.

Balance Living in cattails and tall grasses, these acrobats perch gently on tender stalks.

Red Wings This bird is named for the males' red and yellow shoulder patches. Females are brown.

Robin
(American Robin)

PLACE PLACE PLACE

SIZE FOOD

NEST MIGRATION

Lee Karney, US Fish and Wildlife Service

CLASSIFICATION

SCIENTIFIC NAME
Turdus migratorius

BIRD FAMILY
Thrush family

ROCKY MOUNTAIN RELATIVES
Mountain Bluebird, Hermit Thrush, Swainson's Thrush

HABITAT

NEST
Cup-shaped nests made of grasses are placed in trees or other structures protected from wind and rain.

FOOD
Earthworms, small insects, beetles, grasshoppers, caterpillars and berries.

MIGRATION
To lower elevations within the southwestern states.

THEY'RE EVERYWHERE Robins commonly live near humans in suburban areas making them one of the most commonly observed bird species. They feed most mornings on earthworms in parks and grassy lawns and may nest under covered porches and on exposed beams near houses. These birds, however, do not only live in the suburbs! Robins are equally abundant in forests from low-elevation aspen groves up to subalpine forests near treeline.

ROBIN RED BREAST American Robins are not Robins at all. They are a member of the Thrush family. Early European settlers observed the red-breasted bird and assumed that it was related to the European Robin commonly known there as Robin Red-Breast. The stories and poems written about Robin Red-Breast were written about the European Robin, not our local American Robin.

EARLY BIRDS In the case of the American Robin, it is true that "the early bird gets the worm." Throughout the summer, Robins feed on worms which live near the soil surface in the cool temperatures of dawn. As daytime temperatures warm, worms move deeper below ground where Robins cannot see their activity. For this reason, Robins feed on worms in the early morning, then feed on insects or berries throughout the warmer temperatures of daytime.

family field guide

INDICATOR SPECIES

In summer, Robins eat worms which they find in parks and grassy lawns. Worms which live in poisonous soils absorb the poisons and become toxic food for Robins. Scientists observe Robin populations to determine if urban and suburban areas are overly polluted. Before using toxic fertilizers and weed sprays, be careful to ensure that the amount of poison used will not poison bugs in the grass which are a major food source for birds. Better yet, try using a non-toxic gardening method first!

VISUAL PREDATOR

Robins commonly twist their heads toward the ground as if listening for the sounds of worms squirming below the surface. In fact, they twist their heads to get a better *view* of the soil where they look for tiny underground movements.

EYE RING

Besides the obvious red-breast, the white eye ring is an identifying characteristic of the American Robin.

Forests Robins are common in open forests throughout the mountains.

Suburbs Robins are adapted to surviving in cities, feeding on earthworms in open parks and yards.

Sapsucker
(Red-naped Sapsucker)

PLACE

PLACE

SIZE

FOOD

NEST

MIGRATION

National Park Service

CLASSIFICATION

SCIENTIFIC NAME
Sphyrapicus ruber

BIRD FAMILY
Woodpecker

ROCKY MOUNTAIN RELATIVES
Williamson's Sapsucker, Hairy, Downy and Lewis's Woodpeckers, Northern Flicker

HABITAT

NEST
Peck their own cavities in tree trunks; eggs are laid directly on the wood within the nesting chamber.

FOOD
Tree sap, ants and insects stuck in the sap, seeds and berries.

MIGRATION
To southern United States, Mexico and Central America.

SAP EATERS Sapsuckers are woodpeckers which feed mostly on tree sap. These birds peck small, shallow holes in tree bark allowing the tree sap to ooze to the surface where it is eaten. This feeding strategy is similar to the way people collect the sap of Maple trees for maple syrup.

SAP WELLS After drilling several holes into a tree, Sapsuckers wait nearby while the sap oozes to the surface. These tiny holes fill with sap and are called *sap wells*. Sapsuckers work throughout the day pecking at drying, hardened sap to ensure that fresh sap continues to flow. Sap wells are maintained for a day or so, then, as the sap stops flowing and the well fills with crystallized sugar, the sap well is abandoned.

WINGED THIEVES While Sapsuckers are busy maintaining a feeding site, hummingbirds often sneak in to drink the sap. Hummingbirds commonly nest near sap wells, follow Sapsuckers to their feeding sites and may even time their migrations according to those of Sapsuckers so they can share their sugary food. Sapsuckers work hard to defend their sap wells, but the smaller, faster hummingbirds are often able to sneak in for a sip of the nectar-like food.

IDENTIFICATION The red spot on the back of the head (the *nape*) is unique from Williamson's Sapsucker and the red chin is unique from Hairy and Downy Woodpeckers.

family field guide

TONGUE

Insect-eating woodpeckers have long, sticky tongues for collecting insects. Sapsucker tongues are shorter than other woodpeckers and have hair-like tips, like a paintbrush, for gathering sap.

RELATIVES

For many years, any black and white sapsucker with a red head across the Unites States was called a Yellow-bellied Sapsucker. Recent studies have identified three different species within this group of very similar looking birds: the Yellow-bellied Sapsucker found east of the Rocky Mountains, the Red-naped Sapsucker (found in the Rocky Mountains) and the Red-bellied Sapsucker (found on the west coast). Williamson's Sapsucker also lives in the Rocky Mountains, but males have a yellow breast and no red head feathers.

INSECTS

While sap is the main food supply, insects often get stuck in the sticky wells. These insects become an important source of food for the Sapsuckers and other birds which fly past. Adults collect insects, especially ants, to feed nestlings and fledglings.

SEASONAL FEEDING

In spring, when temperatures are still cool, Sapsuckers drill wells in evergreen and aspen trees. As temperatures warm up in mid-summer, the birds prefer to drill their wells in *deciduous* trees, especially aspen, cottonwood, river birch and mountain alder.

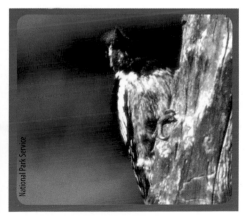

Red Chin Red-naped Sapsuckers have a red chin which is unique from other local woodpeckers.

Sap Wells Sapsuckers punch holes in tree bark, then eat the sap and insects which get stuck in the ooze.

Steller's Jay

PLACE

PLACE

SIZE

FOOD

NEST

MIGRATION

National Park Service

CLASSIFICATION

SCIENTIFIC NAME
Cyanocitta stelleri

BIRD FAMILY
Raven, Magpie and Jay family

ROCKY MOUNTAIN RELATIVES
Raven, Crow, Magpie, Clark's Nutcracker, Scrub Jay, Pinyon Jay, Gray Jay

HABITAT

NEST
Big, cup-shaped nest made from twigs, grasses, moss and leaves held together with mud; placed in evergreen trees.

FOOD
Insects, small rodents, bird eggs, baby birds, small adult birds, seeds, nuts and berries.

MIGRATION
None; some move to lower elevations with less snow.

EASY IDENTIFICATION Steller's Jays vary slightly in color throughout their range. Those living in the Rocky Mountains have dark head and crest feathers and white spots above the eyes. The Steller's Jays in the United States tend to be darker in color than those in Mexico and Central America and those in California tend to have a lighter colored crest and white patches on their chin and throat. All solid blue, crested jays are the same type of bird: the Steller's Jay. Blue Jays, in contrast, have a crest, but also have a white face and white streaks on their wings.

COMPETITION Many different types of Jays live within the Rocky Mountains, but some, including the Steller's Jay, Scrub Jay and Clark's Nutcracker, live in different ecosystems where they do not compete for food. Though their populations overlap in many cases, Steller's Jays tend to live at lower elevations than the Clark's Nutcracker and at higher elevations than the Scrub Jay.

CAMP THIEVES Steller's Jays usually live alone and do not depend on humans for food. Some birds, however, nest near campsites and can become comfortable taking food from people. Please do not feed these birds. Even though they are beautiful and close encounters create magical moments, feeding any type of wildlife turns the wild animals into pests and also contributes to an unhealthy, unnatural diet.

family field guide

GEORGE STELLER

This blue-colored Jay is named after George Steller, a German-born explorer who lead an expedition from Siberia across the Bering Straight. George Steller is best known as the first European to set foot in modern-day Alaska.

PROVINCIAL BIRD

The Steller's Jay is the *provincial* bird of British Columbia, Canada. In Canada, provinces are similar to states, so a provincial bird in Canada is similar to a state bird in the U.S.

VOICE

Like all jays, the Steller's Jay is a noisy bird. It sometimes uses its voice to sound like a Red-tailed Hawk in its effort to scare away predators.

RANGE

Steller's Jays have the widest range of any bird in the Jay family. They live in evergreen forests of western North America from Alaska, south through California and the Rocky Mountains, down through the mountains of Mexico and Central America all the way to Nicaragua!

Evergreens Steller's Jays remain under the cover of evergreen trees throughout winter.

Blue Bright blue wings and back stand out from the dark colored shoulders, head and tail.

Swallows
(Barn, Cliff, Tree and Violet-green)

PLACE • PLACE • PLACE

SIZE • FOOD

NEST • NEST • MIGRATION

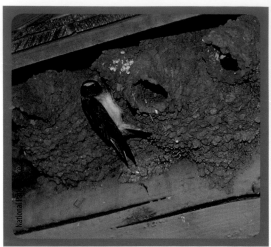

CLASSIFICATION

SCIENTIFIC NAME
Tachycineta bicolor (Tree Swallow)
Tachycineta thalassina (Violet-green Swallow)
Petrochelidon pyrrhonota (Cliff Swallow)
Hirundo rustica (Barn Swallow)

BIRD FAMILY
Swallow and Martin family

ROCKY MOUNTAIN RELATIVES
Northern Rough-winged and Bank Swallows

HABITAT

NEST
Tree and Violet-green Swallows: Tree cavities or small cracks in rocks.
Cliff and Barn Swallows: Gourd-shaped nests made from mud.

FOOD
Almost entirely flying insects.

MIGRATION
South through Mexico, Central and South America.

TWO NESTS Swallows are divided into two different groups based on the type of nests they build. One group of swallows, including the Tree Swallow and the Violet-green Swallow, nest in cavities. The cavities may include abandoned woodpecker holes or man-made nesting boxes. The second group, including the Cliff Swallow and Barn Swallow, collect tiny droplets of mud and patch them together beneath bridges, overhanging cliffs or beneath the eaves of houses. Each nest may require up to 1,500 mud droplets which are collected and placed one at a time.

BUG CONTROL Along with bats, Swallows are considered one of the most important natural predators of flying insects. A healthy Swallow population is important for controlling insect populations. Because of their feeding habits, all Swallows are designed to fly fast and to change direction quickly to keep up with flying insects. Swallows have short, streamlined bodies with long, pointed wings designed for quick turns. Besides turning quickly, Swallows are able to glide at high speeds along the surface of water where they pick up bugs floating on the surface.

COMMUNICATION Swallows are able to make a wide variety of calls to communicate about food, defense and mating. Listen carefully for the quiet chattering among Swallows. They do not make loud calls, but they chatter constantly.

family field guide

BARN SWALLOW

Identification: forked tail and rust-colored belly. Live on all continents of the world except Australia. Populations have increased with human development as they nest in barns, below bridges, dams, and roofs of houses. May form colonies of up to 50 or more nests. Winter in Central and South America.

CLIFF SWALLOW

Identification: a light colored square above the beak. Live in large colonies of between several dozen and several thousand nests where birds "tell" each other about successful feeding areas. Nest beneath manmade structures or overhanging cliffs. Winter in Central and South America.

TREE SWALLOW

Identification: eye *above* the white chin patch. This is the only Swallow which feeds on seeds and berries when insects are less abundant, which allows them to return to Rocky Mountain breeding grounds a month before other Swallows. Winter in southern United States south to Central America.

VIOLET-GREEN SWALLOW

Identification: eye *within* the white cheek patch. Live in abandoned woodpecker holes and commonly use nesting boxes. Populations of both Tree Swallows and Violet-green Swallows have increased with the use of nesting boxes. Winter in Mexico and Central America.

Jacob W. Dingel · PGC Photo

Donna Dewhurst · US Fish and Wildlife Service

Cavity Nests Tree Swallows (above) and Violet-green Swallows nest in tree cavities or nest boxes.

Mud Nests Cliff Swallows (above) and Barn Swallows build mud nests under ledges and roofs.

family field guide

Turkey
(Wild Turkey)

PLACE

SIZE

ADULTS

YOUNG

NEST

MIGRATION

(c) Colorado Division of Wildlife

CLASSIFICATION

SCIENTIFIC NAME
Meleagris gallopovo

BIRD FAMILY
Grouse and Turkey family

ROCKY MOUNTAIN RELATIVES
Blue Grouse and White-tailed Ptarmigan

HABITAT

NEST
Ground nests in hidden depressions near edges of meadows or in open woods.

FOOD
Adults: seeds, grasses, berries and roots.
Young: grasshoppers and other insects.

MIGRATION
Wander short distances to lower elevations in winter.

FLOCKING Turkeys live in four different non-breeding groups in summer, fall and winter. Females with young *poults* live together, mature males live together, "teenage" males live together and females without any young live together. As the daylight hours become longer in spring, the male flocks begin to follow the females. Within weeks, the female flocks break into smaller groupings and the males divide up to follow them. Once breeding season is over in late spring, the flocks join their non-breeding groups again.

BY AIR AND BY LAND Wild Turkeys nest and feed on the ground and they prefer running to flying given the option. They can run up to 18 miles per hour, much faster than the fastest Olympic athletes. If they are startled, however, they fly straight up in the air, a characteristic unique to the Turkey. They flap their wings several times to *roost* in treetops or may coast downhill at high speeds to escape danger.

MATING SEASON Turkey mating season is a fun time to explore ponderosa pine and aspen forests. In April and May, the males (toms) actively attract females (hens). The toms gobble loudly and can be heard nearly 1/2-mile away. Hearing the mating call of Turkeys in spring is a seasonal ritual like elk bugling is the annual call of fall. Males gobble loudly, spread their tail feathers, lengthen their *snoods* and puff up their body feathers in their effort to attract hens.

family field guide

BEN FRANKLIN

While looking at a draft drawing of the first *national seal,* Benjamin Franklin thought the picture looked more like a turkey than an eagle. In response, he wrote a letter to his daughter stating that, "the Turkey is, in comparison, a much more respectable Bird, and a true original Native of America," but he never officially debated that the Turkey should be our nation's symbol. One year before writing this private letter, which has become a lasting legend, Franklin published an article suggesting the rattlesnake as our national symbol.

DECORATIONS

Male turkeys are colorful with many unique body features. A flap of skin called a *snood* hangs over the beak; they can lengthen or shorten the snood to express their mood. The brain-like skin that hangs around their neck is called the *wattle*. The bristle-like feathers growing out from the male's breast is the *beard*. Older Toms have longer beards.

DIET

Young Turkeys, called *poults*, eat mostly grasshoppers and other insects. They need a lot of protein when they are young, but as they get older they increasingly eat more seeds, nuts and grasses. Adult turkeys are almost entirely *herbivorous*.

HUNTED

Turkey hunting season happens twice each year, six weeks in spring and six weeks in fall.

Colorado Division of Wildlife

Display The male Turkey fans its broad tail feathers to attract as many mates as possible in spring.

Colorado Division of Wildlife

Female Female turkeys also have bare red heads, but without the *wattle* or the *snood*.

Vulture
(Turkey Vulture)

 PLACE
 PLACE
 SIZE
 FOOD
 MIGRATION

Jacob Dingel PGC Photo

CLASSIFICATION

SCIENTIFIC NAME
Cathartes aura

BIRD FAMILY
American Vulture family

ROCKY MOUNTAIN RELATIVES
None

HABITAT

NEST
No nest is built; eggs are laid on the ground in caves, large tree cavities, mammal burrows, abandoned barns and other protected areas.

FOOD
Mostly dead animals, but also insects, small rodents and berries.

MIGRATION
South to Mexico, Central and South America.

AN AMERICAN STORK Vultures are commonly mistaken as *birds of prey*, but they are more closely related to storks. *Raptors* catch live prey with their talons while Turkey Vultures eat dead animals with their beaks. Also, like its stork relatives, Turkey Vultures poop on their legs to keep cool on hot days.

SMELL Turkey Vultures depend more on smell than on sight for locating food. Dead animals have a strong odor and Turkey Vultures have a good sense of smell to detect them. Their sense of smell allows them to identify food sources located beneath trees and bushes where their eyes cannot see. Smell is also important to Vultures because their food never moves. Raptors, which depend on their eyes to locate food, look for movement when hunting, but vultures feed on dead animals which do not move and are difficult to locate visually.

SKINHEAD Vulture feeding is very dirty. When eating dead animals, they stick their head deep into *carcasses* which have bugs, maggots and bacteria growing inside. Raptors, which mostly eat fresh meat, only have to deal with blood and guts, but Vultures get dirty with bacteria. A feathered head would be difficult to clean and the birds could become sick from bacteria. Their featherless head is an adaptation to their scavenging lifestyle that allows easy cleaning after each meal.

family field guide

DEAD FOOD

Vultures sometimes eat live baby birds and small reptiles, but they mostly feed on dead animals. They prefer eating animals which have only been dead for a few hours so that the meat is not rotten. Their stomach and intestines, however, are not affected by bacteria and micro-organisms which have been growing on meat for several days.

V-SHAPE

In flight, Vultures lift their wings high in the air creating a V-shape. Hawks and Eagles, by comparison, spread their wings flat. The V-shape allows warm winds to rise without lifting the huge, low-flying wings. The birds sometimes tilt from side to side using their wings to balance against rising air at low altitudes.

WEAK FEET

Unlike *raptors*, Vultures have very weak feet. They are not able to carry food in their feet, so they usually eat their food on the ground where it died.

LOW FLYER

Groups of Turkey Vultures soaring high in the sky are not hunting. When looking for food, Turkey Vultures fly low to the ground and usually fly alone. Low flight allows them to smell dead animals on the ground.

National Park Service

Small Head Golden Eagles and Tukey Vultures have similar wing spans, but Vultures have small heads.

National Park Service

Communal Roost Turkey Vultures roost in large communities, but they usually "hunt" alone.

family field guide

Woodpecker
(Hairy and Downy)

PLACE	PLACE	PLACE
DOWNY	HAIRY	FOOD

NEST	MIGRATION

CLASSIFICATION

SCIENTIFIC NAME
Picoides villosus-Hairy Woodpecker
Picoides pubescens-Downy Woodpecker

BIRD FAMILY
Woodpeckers

ROCKY MOUNTAIN RELATIVES
Lewis's Woodpecker, Northern Flicker, Red-naped Sapsucker

HABITAT

NEST
Peck own cavities in tree trunks; eggs are laid directly on the wood within the nesting chamber.

FOOD
Insects living beneath tree bark.

MIGRATION
None; some move to lower elevations.

VARIATIONS The name Woodpecker refers to a large family of birds, all of which walk up tree trunks and have long beaks for pecking holes. Besides these common features, the appearance and behavior of woodpeckers varies greatly.

FOOD Woodpeckers use many different feeding strategies. Sapsuckers (p. 68) tap holes in tree bark to eat the sap. They return back to the *sap well* to eat trapped insects and occasionally catch flying insects, too. In summer, Flickers (p. 28) mostly eat ants off the ground. In contrast, Hairy and Downy Woodpeckers eat insects and their eggs, almost entirely off of tree trunks and branches. They walk along tree limbs looking and listening for insects in cracks and holes beneath the bark. Once they identify an insect, they use their beak to dig beneath the bark then flick their long, sticky tongue until they catch the helpless insects.

DRUMMING In spring, woodpeckers pound their beaks against hollow logs or other objects to make the loudest noise possible. This behavior, called *drumming*, is used by males to attract mates and to establish territories. Drumming is very fast and is not intended to dig wood out for nest building. Drumming is a unique form of communication to woodpeckers and can be heard nearly 1/4-mile in all directions.

family field guide

BUILT FOR PECKING

Woodpeckers are uniquely designed for climbing and pecking on tree trunks. According to *Sibley's Guide to Bird Life and Behavior*, the bones in the front of their head are folded several times for added thickness which can absorb constant pounding without hurting the brain. Strong muscles behind their bill absorb some of the impact of smashing their mouth into wooden trunks. Their nostrils are narrow and covered with feathers to stop sawdust from getting into their nose. They are able to angle their toes so that two are up and two are down which provides extra pounding support. Finally, they have stiff tail feathers which they press against the tree providing support and leverage for pounding. Woodpecker beaks, bones, toes and tails are all designed for pecking.

FANCY TONGUE

Woodpecker tongues are long, sticky and have tiny hooks at the ends, all of which are useful in capturing bugs from cracks or deep holes. Their tongues are so long that they coil down into their throats and up around their eye and can extend up to 5 inches beyond the tip of their beak when extended. Imagine touching the top of your forehead with your tongue! Their tongues are attached to several complex bones and muscles which flex and shift upward thrusting the tongue forward quickly enough to capture fast-moving insects.

IDENTIFICATION

Hairy and Downy Woodpeckers look similar, but Hairies are the size of a softball and Downies are the size of a baseball.

Downy Woodpecker These small birds feed from small branches. Males have a red spot on their head, females do not.

Hairy Woodpecker Hairy Woodpeckers are much larger than Downies. Males have a red spot on their head, females do not.

family field guide

Nests

CUP-SHAPED NEST

Bald Eagle Osprey
Cedar Waxwing Great-horned Owl
Clark's Nutcracker Raven
Dipper Red-tailed Hawk
Golden Eagle Red-winged Blackbird
Gray Jay Robin
Great Blue Heron Steller's Jay
Hummingbird Cliff Swallow
Magpie Barn Swallow

CAVITY NEST

Chickadee
Flicker
Kingfisher
Mountain Bluebird
Nuthatch
Sapsucker
Tree Swallow
Violet-green Swallow
Woodpeckers

GROUND NEST

Coot
Goose
Grouse
Mallard
Meadowlark
Ptarmigan
Turkey

CUP-SHAPED NESTS

Most people think of nests as cup-shaped structures built of grasses, sticks and mud. These nests, however, vary dramatically in size and construction material. Hummingbirds build cup-shaped nests that can fit into the palm of a hand while Bald Eagles use the same design, but their nests are as large as a person's bedroom. Magpies add a top to their nests for extra protection.

CAVITY NESTS

Nesting cavities are dug into trees or soft, muddy cliffs. Beyond the tiny entrance, a nesting chamber is carved that is large enough to hold a small family. Woodpeckers are the most important cavitiy builders, but many other species use their abandoned nests. Kingfishers and several Swallow species dig cavities into muddy cliff walls.

GROUND NESTS

Birds that are not good fliers like Blue Grouse, Ptarmigan and Wild Turkey do not depend on flight to access their nests. Instead, they build nests on the ground. These nests are in constant danger of predators like coyotes, foxes and pine martens, so the nests are hidden beneath tall grasses, dense shrubs or fallen trees. Ducks and geese usually nest on the ground near water.

family field guide

BREEDING SEASON ONLY Bird nests are one of the most interesting and misunderstood parts of bird behavior. Most noteably, nests are only used while *incubating* eggs and raising *nestlings* (young, flightless birds). Once nestlings leave the nest, the nest is abandoned for the season. Some birds, however, use the same nest to lay several sets of eggs in a single season. Similarly, some birds return to use the same nest every year for many years.

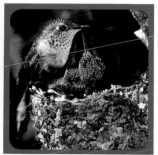

PURPOSE

Birds build nests to lay their eggs and to raise their young until they are old enough to fly. Once the young birds can fly, the nests are abandoned. Some birds lay several sets of eggs during the summer, so their nests are used for several months. Any bird that is not busy *incubating* eggs or learning to fly does not use a nest, so most of the year, birds do not use nests for shelter.

SAFETY

Nests must provide safety from predators, so most are well hidden. Some are placed in tall tree tops, others are camouflaged beneath grasses or in thick shrubs. Nests that are easy to see, like those of Barn and Cliff Swallows (left), are placed on cliff ledges where predators are not likely to reach them. Some birds, like the Nuthatch, mask their smell by dusting animal hair or insect guts around their nesting hole so that predators will not smell them.

LOCATION

The location of nests varies widely among birds. The least complex nests are scraped into the dirt and are built by birds that do not depend on flight. The most complex and hard-to-reach nests are built by birds that are the best flyers, the Swallows. Most birds place their nests in areas that best suit their lifestyle. For example, birds that are adapted to climb on trees, nest in trees, birds that depend on water, nest near water.

WARMTH

Nests are designed to help keep eggs warm. For this reason, most birds use grasses, hair, feathers and other materials which maintain warmth against wind and cold temperatures. Woodpeckers, however, do not use such materials. Instead, they peck nesting cavities (holes) into the south or west-facing sides of tree trunks so that daytime sun rays help to keep the nest warm.

Migration

ROCKY MOUNTAIN MIGRATIONS

The migration pattern of many species varies between individuals. For example, some Mallards remain in the Montane life zone throughout winter, but many choose to migrate hundreds of miles to warmer climates. For this reason, many birds are listed in two different migration categories.

NONE

Bald Eagle	Kingfisher
Chickadee	Magpie
Clark's Nutcracker	Mallard
Dipper	Nuthatch
Flicker	Ptarmigan
Goose	Raven
Gray Jay	Steller's Jay
Great-horned Owl	Turkey
Grouse	Woodpeckers

REGIONAL

Bald Eagle
Cedar Waxwing
Coot
Golden Eagle
Goose
Great Blue Heron
Kingfisher
Magpie
Mallard
Meadowlark
Mountain Bluebird
Osprey
Red-tailed Hawk
Red-winged Blackbird
Robin

NEO-TROPICAL

Cedar Waxwing
Hummingbird
Swallows
Turkey Vulture
Sapsucker

WINTER GROUNDS AND BREEDING GROUNDS

All animals want to raise their young in the best possible conditions in spring, but they also need food all year long. Birds have the luxury of flight, so they are able to move anywhere in the world to find a good spring home for raising a family (breeding range) and a winter home that provides food (winter range) too.

NAVIGATION

Scientists and casual observers have long wondered how birds can fly long distances and arrive at the exact same winter and breeding grounds every year. Scientists believe that they use three different tools for navigation: the sun, the stars and the earth's magnetic field. Daytime migrants use the sun to tell direction, nighttime migrants use the stars and all birds have tiny grains of a mineral called *magnetite* located just above their beak which may act like a compass allowing them to "feel" the northern pull of the earth's magnetic field.

MIGRATION PREPARATION

Migrating birds must tune their bodies before long migrations. First, they need to store extra energy. Birds eat large amounts of food during the weeks leading up to migration which is used to store extra fat. The fat is used as energy during their long flights. Second, they make sure their feathers are working just right. Most will replace old and worn out feathers with new, healthy ones in the weeks before migration.

DANGERS OF MIGRATION

Unlike mammals, birds have the ability to move thousands of miles to find the best feeding grounds throughout the year. Migrations, however, require lots of energy and sometimes involve dangerous encounters with weather, predators, buildings, power lines and cars. Storms often blow birds over open water or other barren landscapes that do not provide food or safe landing. Also, birds that are exhausted from their long flights are easy targets for predators.

LENGTH

Migrations vary dramatically in their length. Most birds require several weeks, stopping in *staging areas*, or *stopover sites*, along the way. Birds remain in the staging areas for several days to rest and eat before continuing to their destination. Some migrations, however, are completed very quickly. Broad-tailed Hummingbirds, which migrate up to 400 miles, complete their trip in a non-stop, 24-hour flight.

DAYTIME AND NIGHTTIME

Raptors, insect eaters and water birds usually migrate during the day. Raptors depend on warm, rising air to help them fly more efficiently, so they wait until the warmth of day to migrate. Insect eaters, like Swallows, migrate during the day when insects are active so they can eat along the way. Water birds fly during the day, then roost at night in the safety of open lakes. In contrast, most small songbirds feed during the day and migrate at night.

Bird Food: Plants

All together, birds feed on almost every food source imaginable. Besides large mammals and poisonous foods, every animal, plant, insect and spider is a possible food for some type of bird. Even leftover human food is eaten by *scavengers*.

SEEDS

Seeds contain a lot of energy and are a main food source for many birds. Most seed-eaters have short, powerful beaks for crushing hard shells. While seeds are important in summer and fall, they are covered by snow in winter. Many seed-eating birds either migrate in winter or use foods that they collected and stored in the fall. Wintering birds may depend on bird feeders, so winter feeders should be kept full all season.

WATER PLANTS

Rivers, lakes and creeks are filled with many different types of plants. These plants are an important part of the food chain for water birds including Coots, ducks and geese. Canada Geese, Mallards and other "dabbling" birds eat plants from the water's surface or in shallow bottoms, while Coots and other "diving" birds are able to dive underwater to eat plants from deeper parts of lakes.

BERRIES

Berries are an important food source in late summer, fall and winter. They provide a lot of energy for birds preparing for migration in late summer, are a high-energy snack at *stopover sites* during fall migration and are an important food throughout winter even after they have dried up like raisins.

EVERGREEN SEEDS

Evergreen trees store seeds in cones. Most of these seeds form in late fall and are an important pre-migration food for migrating birds and are winter food for non-migrating birds.

PINE NEEDLES AND LEAVES

Most birds do not eat pine needles or leaves. Plants store most of their energy in seeds and berries, so these are the most important plant foods for most birds. Some birds, however, eat needles and leaves when other foods are not available.

family field guide

Bird Food: Animals

INSECTS, LARVAE, EGGS AND SPIDERS

Insects are more diverse and abundant than any other type of animal and are an important source of food for many birds. Whether in flight, under water, beneath tree bark, in dead trees or hidden in thick grasses, all insects are prey for some type of bird. Even in winter, when most insects are *dormant*, their eggs and *larvae* are food for woodpeckers.

FISH

Birds are one of the primary predators of fish in the Rocky Mountain region. Shallow-swimming fish are food for Kingfishers, Great Blue Herons, Osprey and Bald Eagles. These four birds combine to eat fish of all sizes. Kingfishers and Herons swallow the fish whole, while the raptors use their beaks to eat them one bite at a time.

EGGS AND NESTLINGS

Parent birds work hard to hide their nests, eggs and *fledglings*. Even with camouflage, hidden nests and other defenses, eggs, baby birds and roosting songbirds often become food for predators. Birds of prey and most members of the Jay family (Magpies, Ravens, Nutcrackers, Gray Jays, etc.) are common predators of baby birds and eggs.

AQUATIC INSECTS

Many insects begin their life under rocks in rivers, lakes and wetlands. These underwater bugs are important food for Dippers and many types of water birds. As the insects grow, they develop wings and rise up to the surface. The insects dry off on blades of grass or dry rocks before they can fly. During this resting stage they are food for many hungry birds. Once they begin flying, they become prey for Swallows, the second most important animal in controlling insect populations next to bats.

SMALL ANIMALS

Mice, voles, moles, rabbits and hares are the main food source for most *raptors*. Snakes and amphibians are also important foods. Because they don't have teeth, raptors use sharp talons to capture their prey and a sharp beak to tear the meat into bite-sized pieces. The smallest of animals are eaten whole.

family field guide

Lowland Shrub and Forest

WHAT IS THE LOWLAND SHRUB AND FOREST?

The hills, valleys and pastures that make up this life zone are often called the "foothills." This life zone ranges from 6,000 to 8,000 feet above sea level or up to 9,000 feet above sea level on south-facing slopes. It is most easily identified by the presence of Pinyon Pines, Junipers, Gambel Oak and Sagebrush.

EARLY ARRIVALS

Spring weather arrives earlier to this life zone than to those at higher elevations, so some migratory birds including the Red-winged Blackbird, arrive to these habitats as early as February, but most species arrive in March or April. By comparison, migratory birds do not arrive to the Subalpine or Alpine life zones until June.

SEASONAL WEATHER

This is the hottest and driest of all life zones in the Rocky Mountains. Because of the relatively low elevation, daytime temperatures here are generally warmer than the higher life zones. These warm temperatures melt the snow by mid-April, and dry out the grasses by early July. Seeds are abundant throughout late summer and into fall and the winter is much less severe than at higher elevations. The mild climate and diverse ecosystems support a variety of bird species.

WINTER DESTINATION

Winter conditions are less severe here than in higher elevations. Snow does not accumulate to such depths as in the higher elevations. Waterways often remain clear of snow and ice, allowing water birds and fish eaters to remain through winter. In open pastures, however, snow is deep enough to cover the homes of burrowing rodents, so most Golden Eagles and Red-tailed Hawks migrate to pastures in lower elevations.

BIRDS COMMON TO THIS LIFE ZONE

Cedar Waxwing, Chickadees, Flicker, Golden Eagle, Hummingbirds, Magpie, Meadowlark, Mountain Bluebird, Nuthatches, Great-horned Owl, Raven, Red-tailed Hawk, Red-winged Blackbird, Robin, Sapsuckers, Swallows, Turkey Vulture, Woodpeckers

family field guide

FIVE ECOSYSTEMS, ONE LIFE ZONE

This life zone includes Pinyon/Juniper woodlands, Sage flats, Scrub Oak, dry pastures and riparian areas. These ecosystems combined support a diverse population of bird species.

SCRUB OAK

A dense thicket of shrubs including Gambel Oak, Serviceberry and Mountain Mahogany creates a tangled web of dense branches on low-elevation foothills. These dense, shrubby thickets provide excellent protection for nesting birds. The berry bushes and acorns provide food while dried grasses provide nesting material for songbirds.

PINYON/JUNIPER WOODLANDS

Pinyon/Juniper forests typically grow in dry, rocky soil. Fewer grasses and wildflowers grow among these drought tolerant evergreens than in other ecosystems. In summer, when temperatures are hot and plants have formed seeds, seed-eating birds scratch the ground for food and raptors soar overhead looking for chipmunks and rabbits. Some birds migrate here in winter to feed on Pinyon nuts and Juniper berries.

SAGEBRUSH FLATS

Sagebrush flats are home to a host of small mammals which are food for soaring raptors. Because there are few trees or dense shrubs for hiding, most nesting birds here are ground-nesting birds like the Western Meadowlark. The primary attraction to these open, grassy flats is for soaring raptors which hunt rabbits, mice and other small mammals.

PASTURES AND HAY FIELDS

Grasses grow tall and dense in low-elevation pastures which are commonly hayed by ranchers for winter cattle feed. These grasslands are home to caterpillars, beetles and thousands of insects which provide food for Meadowlarks, Mountain Bluebirds and other *insectivores*. Immediately after grasses have been cut for hay, Magpies and Robins flock to eat the exposed insects, as well. Raptors prey on the abundant mice and voles.

Montane Life Zone

WHERE IS THE MONTANE LIFE ZONE?

The Montane life zone occurs from 8,000-10,000 feet above sea level. Summer conditions here last from June to October, allowing just enough time for migrating birds to nest and raise their young before the snow flies. Many resort towns and mining towns have developed in this elevation range, so interactions between humans and wildlife are common.

BIRDS AND BEARS

Large populations of humans are rapidly moving to Montane life zones. Many aspects of increased human development harm wildlife habitats, but in some ways they attract wildlife, as well. For example, increased garbage often attracts bears into towns and bird feeders attract bears into peoples' yards. It is important to remove bird feeders in the spring and fall when bears are hungriest!

FEEDING WILDLIFE

Montane forests and meadows are common hiking and camping destinations for hikers, campers, skiers and more. Gray Jays are a popular highlight among picnickers in the upper reaches of the Montane life zone. Though these and other birds commonly beg for food, please do not feed wildlife, even if they wait politely nearby. Also, be careful to pick up all food remains from camp sites and picnic grounds to prevent accidental feedings. Feeding wildlife creates an unnatural diet and can create wildlife pests.

BIRDS COMMON TO THIS LIFE ZONE

Cedar Waxwing, Chickadees, Clark's Nutcracker, Flicker, Golden Eagle, Gray Jay, Grouse, Hummingbirds, Magpie, Meadowlark, Mountain Bluebird, Nuthatches, Great-horned Owl, Raven, Red-tailed Hawk, Red-winged Blackbird, Robin, Sapsucker, Steller's Jay, Swallows, Turkey, Turkey Vulture, Woodpeckers

family field guide

FIVE ECOSYSTEMS, ONE LIFE ZONE

The Montane life zone consists of aspen groves, dry meadows, lodgepole and ponderosa pine forests, douglas fir forests and riparian ecosystems. These ecosystems combined with a long summer season, create diverse habitat for a variety of birds.

LODGEPOLE PINE FORESTS

These tall, straight tree trunks are excellent nesting posts for cavity nesting birds and the dead and fallen trees are protection for ground-nesting birds. Ground cover plants and seed-producing grasses are food for ground nesting birds like Wild Turkeys and Blue Grouse.

DRY MEADOWS

Most birds in the Montane life zone nest in aspen and evergreen forests and visit dry meadows for feeding. Many insects, wildflowers and grasses thrive in these grasslands along with small mammals which provide food for soaring hawks and Golden Eagles. Mountain Bluebirds and other insect eaters perch on neighboring tree branches and fence posts to pick insects out of the air or among the grasses in these open fields.

DOUGLAS FIR FORESTS

Douglas fir forests are shadier and more lush than lodgepole and ponderosa pine forests. Douglas fir trees require moist soil and a cooler climate which often supports more abundant plant life on the forest floor. A diversity in plant life leads to more insect life and a richer food chain than drier evergreen forests. Many birds find shelter in the evergreen branches and plenty of food among the shady forest and neighboring meadows.

ASPEN GROVES

Aspen forests support the second greatest diversity of birds next to riparian ecosystems. Sunlight shines through the leaves onto the moist soil allowing tall grasses, wildflowers and berry-producing shrubs to grow up from the forest floor. These plants provide food and nesting material from early summer through fall. Aspen branches provide platforms for cup-shaped nests and the soft woody trunks are favorites for cavity-nesting birds.

Subalpine Life Zone

WHAT IS THE SUBALPINE LIFEZONE?

The Subalpine life zone occurs from 10,000 feet above sea level up to treeline. It consists of enormous evergreen forests, rocky *talus slopes*, wet and dry meadows and riparian ecosystems along small creeks and lakes. Because of the limited ecosystem diversity and the short summer conditions, fewer birds nest in this high altitude environment than at lower elevations, but many birds roost and feed in these shady forests and sunny meadows.

WINTER FOOD

Winter weather arrives early to this high-mountain life zone. Snow begins falling in October and does not melt until late May or June, so most plants are covered for 8 months of each year. Most of the birds that live here in the summer migrate to lower elevations in winter. Those that remain (Clark's Nutcracker, Gray Jay, Chickadee) gather food in fall and use it to survive through winter.

WET MEADOWS

Wet meadows may occur in all life zones, but they are especially common at high elevations where snow melts slowly and soils remain damp throughout the summer. Wildflowers and tall grasses are a sign of boggy ground and, if it gets boggy enough, the meadow may become littered with willows. Tangled willow branches provide safety from predators.

SPRUCE/FIR FORESTS

Subalpine forests are shady and support a limited diversity of ground plants and wild flowers. For this reason, many birds nest and roost in the branches of evergreen trees and visit neighboring meadows or lower elevation aspen groves for midday feeding. While wildflowers are less abundant in the shady forest, several ground cover plants are food for Blue Grouse and other ground dwelling birds. Insects on the trees, in the air and the soil are food for insect-eating birds.

BIRDS COMMON TO THIS LIFE ZONE

Chickadees, Clark's Nutcracker, Flicker, Golden Eagle, Gray Jay, Grouse, Hummingbirds, Great-horned Owl, Raven, Red-tailed Hawk, Robin, Steller's Jay, Swallows, Woodpeckers

family field guide

Alpine Life Zone

WHAT IS THE ALPINE LIFE ZONE?

The Alpine life zone occurs above treeline. It is the least diverse life zone of all. It consists of wet meadows, dry meadows and rocky *talus slopes*. Dense willow thickets provide food and nesting along the banks of creeks and wet meadows. Grasses provide seeds and nesting material in the dry meadows. Because of the open pasture-like environment, Golden Eagles and soaring Hawks commonly hunt these high mountains in summer.

FOOD AND SHELTER

Snow covers most of the ground from October through June, so much of the food and nesting material is hidden for nine months of each year. Even in summer, when the snow is melted and food supplies are abundant, there are no trees to protect birds from weather or predators. For these reasons, most of the birds here are migratory and stay for only a short time. Many birds spend the day here gathering food, then return to the protection of the subalpine forest at night.

OPEN SPACE

The Alpine life zone is a vast, treeless area. Many birds nest in the forests below, and spend their days hunting for insects, worms, nectar and seeds in the vast meadows, rocky slopes, cliffs and lakes of the alpine tundra. Cliff-loving raptors commonly roost on protected cliff ledges where they can easily take flight above this treeless domain in search of Marmot, Pica and other unsuspecting mammals.

TALUS SLOPES

Hillsides full of rock are common in Subalpine and Alpine life zones where freezing water cracks bits of rock from the mountainous cliffs above. These rock fields, or *talus slopes*, are shelter for small mammals called Pica and Marmot. Soaring hawks hunt these mammals in the talus fields which border grassy meadows. Insect-eaters may perch on the rock piles and watch for bugs in neighboring grasses.

BIRDS COMMON TO THIS LIFE ZONE

Ptarmigan, Golden Eagle, Gray Jay, Clark's Nutcracker, Hummingbirds

Riparian Ecosystem

RIPARIAN ECOSYSTEM

Riparian ecosystems are based around water. They include the plants, animals and soils on the edges of creeks, rivers, lakes and wetlands. Because water flows from the Alpine life zone downhill, riparian ecosystems occur in every life zone.

DIVERSITY

An estimated 75% of all birds use riparian ecosystems at some time in their lives. Riparian areas support more plant types than any other ecosystem in the Rocky Mountains. These different plant varieties provide nesting materials, nesting sites, seeds, berries and insects, all of which support many different types of birds. The water itself supports aquatic insects and fish. Fish eaters, insect eaters and seed eaters can all survive here and even birds that don't depend on the water itself nest in the many different tree types that grow along the water's edge.

LARGE RIVERS

Large rivers and the surrounding river bottoms provide habitat for both fish-eating and insect-eating birds. Hatching insects fly up from the water's surface and are a favorite hunting ground for Swallows. Bridges that span the river beds create excellent nesting platforms for Swallows, Kingfishers and Dippers. The shallow edges of rivers are primary hunting grounds for Great Blue Herons, while larger fish eaters snatch fish from the middle of the river currents.

LAKES

Shallow mountain lakes are home to ducks, geese and other water birds. Plants growing on the bottom of ponds and lakes are food for ducks, coots and geese, and the fish, frogs and salamanders are food for water-loving carnivores. Most water birds nest along protected shorelines and depend on the security of open water for nighttime roosting.

NESTING BIRDS IN THIS ECOSYSTEM

Bald Eagle, Coot, Dipper, Goose, Great Blue Heron, Kingfisher, Mallard, Osprey and many more.

family field guide

RIPARIAN DIVERSITY

Wetlands, Cottonwood and Blue Spruce forests, lakes, rivers and creeks are all unique riparian areas based around water. Each area provides unique habitat features for birds, plants and mammals.

WETLANDS

Two main plant communities in wetlands are dense thickets of willows and cattail-filled marshes. These wetland plant communities support a greater diversity and abundance of birds than any other ecosystem. They are especially important for migrating birds which hide in willows and cattails during migrations. The dense growth of plants and the wet, soggy ground provides hiding from all types of predators.

COTTONWOOD FORESTS

Cottonwood forests along river beds provide safety from ground predators as tree nesting birds can perch 20-80 feet in the air. Bald Eagles, Osprey and Great Blue Herons commonly nest in Cottonwood trees so that their hunting grounds are close to home. Bald Eagles, Kingfishers and Osprey often hunt from the long branches of Cottonwood trees before diving for their prey.

BLUE SPRUCE FORESTS

Blue Spruce trees like the water-soaked soil around creeks and rivers. These shady forests provide shelter for nesting birds and small mammals alike. Like the cattails and willows that provide protection in the wetlands, Spruce trees offer similar safety from predators, and they tower up to 100 feet above the ground. Because of their height, even Great Blue Herons sometimes nest in these towering riparian forests.

HIGH MOUNTAIN CREEKS

As snow melts and drains downhill, water fills high mountain creeks. These fast-moving water drainages are much smaller than rivers, but are equally important for providing habitat for birds, plants and mammals. Wetlands, Cottonwoods, Blue Spruce forests all may grow around these fast-moving creeks as well as tall grasses and wildflowers.

Glossary

Aquatic Plants or animals that live or grow in water.

Asymmetrical Two items which are offset from a center line so that the features on the left side do not line up equally with the features on the right.

Bird of prey Birds with talons that eat other animals as their main food source; examples include eagles, hawks, owls and Osprey.

Beard Whiskery feathers growing from a male turkey's breast. The longer the beard, the older the tom.

Brood A group of young birds that are hatched at one time and are cared for by the same mother.

Carcass The body of a dead animal.

Carnivore An animal that eats meat as its main food source.

Carrion Dead or decaying animals.

Cavity A hole dug out of a tree trunk or muddy bank that is used for nesting.

Cellulose The main material in cell walls of most plants.

Contour feathers The feathers that cover a bird's body.

DDT A chemical used in the mid-1900s to kill insects. Its chemical name is Dichloro-Diphenyl-Tri-chloroethane.

Dabbling duck Ducks which feed in shallow water and are unable to dive beneath the water surface; includes many ducks, geese and swans.

Deciduous A tree or shrub which loses its leaves in winter.

Dominance A situation where one animal gains control over another animal.

Dormant To become inactive, especially during winter or periods of cold weather.

Down feathers A layer of fine feathers which grow close to the skin beneath the contour feathers; used primarily for warmth.

Drake A male Mallard.

Drumming The mating call of male woodpeckers made by pounding their beak against hollow logs, siding or other noisy materials.

Eyrie The nest of a bird of prey built in high tree tops. Also spelled aerie.

Fetus The unborn young of an animal.

Fledge When a baby bird first leaves the nest.

Fledgling A young bird that has recently learned to fly, but is still in the care of a parent.

Forest hawks Birds of prey in the hawk family which live and hunt in evergreen forests and feed mostly on songbirds; includes Cooper's and Sharp-shinned Hawks and Northern Goshawk.

Frugivore An animal that feeds mostly on fruits and berries.

Gaping Behavior used by Meadowlarks where the beak is poked into tangled grasses where it prys apart an opening so that it can find hiding insects.

Gorget A patch of colorful feathers on the throat of a bird.

Gosling A baby goose.

Habituate To take or use commonly; to form a habit.

Hawking A feeding strategy used by some birds to catch insects in mid-flight.

Hen A female Mallard and Turkey.

Herbivore An animal that eats mainly plant material.

Herbivorous An animal that eats mainly plant material.

Heronry A colony of nests used by Great Blue Herons.

Incubate To keep eggs or fetuses in a safe, warm environment.

Insectivore An animal that eats mainly insects, spiders or their eggs.

Larva The wingless and often wormlike hatchling of an insect.

Lichen A plant-like growth on tree bark or rocks, composed of a fungus and an algae.

Magnetite A mineral that is naturally magnetic and is made mostly of iron oxide.

Mollusk Animals that have soft bodies within a shell such as clams and snails.

Molt To shed old feathers which are then replaced with new ones.

Mutualism A relationship between two living things in which both of them receive something good.

Nape The back of the neck, usually extending from the shoulders to the back of the skull.

National Seal A symbol that represents a country.

Nestling A young bird which is not yet able to fly.

Nocturnal To sleep during the day and become active at night.

Omnivore An animal that eats both plants and animals.

Opportunist An animal that eats the most common or easily found source of food.

Pigment A colorful material found in cells which creates color in skin, feathers, fur and more.

Plumage The feathers of a bird.

Poult A young turkey.

Provincial Refers to a province of Canada which is similar to a state in the U.S.

Raptor A bird which has talons and eats meat; includes eagles, hawks, owls and Osprey.

Riparian The area along the bank of a river, lake or wetland.

Roost A perch where a bird rests or sleeps; usually protected from wind and weather.

Sap wells Holes punched in tree bark which become filled with tree sap.

Scavenger An animal which commonly feeds on dead animals.

Snood A flap of skin at the upper base of the beak in some birds, especially the turkey.

Soaring hawks Birds of prey in the hawk family which soar over open grasslands and feed mostly on small mammals; includes Red-tailed, Ferruginous, Rough-legged and Swainson's Hawks.

Staging area An area where migrating birds stop to rest and feed either before or during migration.

Stopover site An area where migrating birds stop to rest and feed either before or during migration.

Submissiveness Letting another animal take control.

Talus slope A large pile of rocky boulders which collects at the base of cliffs.

Wattle A flap of bare skin that hangs beneath the chin of some birds; especially the turkey.

Index

family field guide

References

Beletsky, Les. *Bird Songs: 250 North American Birds in Song.* Chronicle Books. 2006.

Burnie, David. *Bird. (Eyewitness Books).* Alfred A. Knopf. 1988.

Cornell Lab of Ornithology. *All About Birds.* Cornell University. 2003.
www.birds.cornell.edu/allaboutbirds/birdguide/

Davis, Kate. *Raptors of the Rockies.* Mountain Press Publishing Company. 2002.

Forshaw, Joseph. [et al.]. *Birding.* Time-Life Books. 1994.

Furtman, Michael. *Why Birds Do That.* Willow Creek Press. 2004.

Gray, Mary Taylor. *The Guide To Colorado Birds.* Westcliffe Publishers. 1998.

Huggins, Janis Lindsey. *Wild at Heart: A Natural History Guide.* Town of Snowmass Village. 2004.

Johnsgard, Paul A. [et al.]. *The Wonder of Birds.* The National Geographic Society. 1983.

Maryjo, Koch. *Bird, Egg, Feather, Nest.* Collins Publishers San Francisco. 1994.

National Geographic Society. *Field Guide to the Birds of North America.* National Geographic. 1999.

Sibley, David. *The Sibley Guide to Bird Life & Behavior.* Alfred A. Knopf Publishing. 2001.

Terres, John K. *The Audubon Society Encyclopedia of North American Birds.* Knopf Publishing. 1980.

Vanner, Michael. *The Encyclopedia of North American Birds.* Barnes & Noble Books. 2003.

About the Author

Garrick taught environmental education at the Aspen Center for Environmental Studies (ACES) for four years, taught high school science in the African kingdom of Lesotho with the U.S. Peace Corps, taught elementary school at the Aspen Community School for three years and currently teaches middle school Language Arts. He continues to teach environmental education courses in the summer months. He lives with his wife, Lindsay, and their son Mason in Basalt, CO.

About the Illustrator

Hilary is an artist, a naturalist, and an educator. Some of her earliest memories are of wearing smocks and painting at easels in pre-school in West Lafayette, IN. Her passion for the visual arts has been lifelong. She is an illustrator and mixed media artist who has worked in photography, oil painting, textiles, printmaking and papermaking. She previously sold enameled jewelry with bold colors and geometric designs. In addition, she works in the field of scientific illustration. Hilary has been an educator for the past ten years. With degrees in both biology and art education she has taught environmental education, guided adventure trips and taught visual arts at the K-12 level. She has been teaching art to K-8th grade students at the Aspen Communtiy School for five years. She also teaches at Anderson Ranch during the summer. Hilary lives in Basalt, CO.

family field guide

family field guide
— SERIES —

field notes

field notes

family field guide